THE BLACK AND ETHNIC MINORITY WOMAN MANAGER:

CRACKING THE CONCRETE CEILING

Marilyn J. Davidson is Senior Lecturer in Organisational Psychology in the Manchester School of Management at the University of Manchester Institute of Science and Technology. She is author of 13 books on women at work, women in management and occupational stress, and two of her most recent books include Paul Chapman publications: *Shattering the Glass Ceiling – The Woman Manager* (with C. L. Cooper) and *Women in Management – Current Research Issues* (edited with R. Burke). She has written over a hundred academic articles, is former Editor of the journal, *Women in Management Review*, Associate Editor of the *Journal of Occupational and Organizational Psychology*, as well as a member of the Editorial Board on the *Journal of Gender Work and Organization* and the *International Review of Women and Leadership*. She has appeared on numerous television and radio programmes, and is a Fellow of the British Psychological Society and Royal Society of Arts.

THE BLACK AND ETHNIC MINORITY WOMAN MANAGER:

CRACKING THE CONCRETE CEILING

by
Marilyn J. Davidson
Manchester School of Management
University of Manchester
Institute of Science and Technology

P·C·P
Paul Chapman
Publishing Ltd

Copyright © 1997, M. J. Davidson

Paul Chapman Publishing Ltd
144 Liverpool Road
London
N1 1LA

British Library Cataloguing in Publication Data
Davidson, Marilyn J.
The black and ethnic minority woman manager:
cracking the concrete ceiling
1. Minority women executives
I. Title
658.4'09
ISBN 1–85396–299–6

Typeset by Whitelaw & Palmer Ltd, Glasgow
Printed and bound in Great Britain

A B C D E F G H   9 8 7

Contents

7. **Positive Approaches to Helping Black and Ethnic Minority**
   Women into Management   98
   • Strategies for Success • What Organisations Can Do – The
   Management of Diversity • Black and Ethnic Minority Workers and
   Trade Unions • Race and Equal Opportunities – Changing the Law
   • Our Children, The Future and Changing Societal Attitudes
   • Conclusions

Preface

My job as Chairwoman of the Equal Opportunities Commission has led me to develop a great understanding and insight into the lives of women, not just in the UK but also in a number of other countries. Equality issues are very important to me and I can trace my interest back to the discrimination I have experienced in my own life.

In 1978 when I came out of Law School looking for my first job I was well qualified, very confident, ambitious, ready to launch myself on the world. Anybody and everybody who knew me said I would have no problems. I applied for 250 jobs at a time when there was a great shortage of newly qualified graduates applying for articles. I didn't get one.

I remember going through a very analytical process based on my training as a lawyer. Was it my dress, my presentation, my interview skills? I couldn't understand it until I faced the stark realisation that it was either gender or race discrimination and I personally found this very shocking.

Discrimination is insidious. It saps your confidence and your self-esteem. It bars you from tried and tested career paths, irrespective of your ability and qualifications. Not unnaturally, I deplore it.

I was therefore very pleased when, in 1994, the Equal Opportunities Commission published two reports which revealed the extent of the double discrimination black and ethnic minority women face on the grounds of race and sex discrimination. It exploded the myth that women are a homogenous group with similar needs and experiences. The Commission used these reports to raise the profile of the issues and to persuade other organisations to develop strategies to deal with them.

Eradicating discrimination is not an easy task. Prejudice and tradition are not lightly swept aside. Dr Davidson's book provides an insight into just how deep-seated the problems are and makes positive and excellent suggestions for the future. The book lends further support for the need for organisational and policy changes to help remedy and eliminate discrimination so that opportunity is available to all. I welcome its publication.

Kamlesh Bahl
Chairwoman
Equal Opportunities Commission

Dedications and Acknowledgements

This book is dedicated to my children, Fern and Lloyd, and to Bob Cooke.

Special thanks to Caroline Davey for her help with interviews and data analysis; fellow researcher, Linda Hite, for her invaluable comments and suggestions on the first book draft; and the Sundridge Park Research Fund for financing this study. Finally, I wish to thank all those women managers who participated in this project and gave their time and energy to share their experiences.

1

The Black and Ethnic Minority Woman Manager – An Overview

On a macro-societal level, (gendered) racism operates through various mechanisms. Black women are (a) marginalised, (b) culturally problematised and (c) impeded in social mobility. They encounter paternalism, they are underestimated, their work is ethnicised, and they generally have fewer career opportunities than men and white women, respectively. These mechanism operate simultaneously and probably stimulate each other.

(Essed, 1991)

INTRODUCTION

Colette (not her real name) is 28 years of age, single, an Afro-Caribbean graduate junior manager. She works in a section of Social Services and was born in the UK. However, the problems and pressures Colette experienced as the first ethnic minority woman to hold her position in a predominantly white company, in the end, forced her to quit her job:

> My career is very important, perhaps too important. I feel terrible now that I have left the company but the job took over my life. I could never switch off. It initially felt strange being the boss because the people who worked for me tended to be older and had been in the company longer. They resented me. What made matters worse was that although I was supposedly in a position of power, my male (white) superiors had ensured in reality, I had no real power. This obviously made my situation impossible and undermined my authority. Nothing was done to enhance my career and I wasn't even given adequate training. Having to deal with racism was also a problem, it wasn't just directed towards me but often towards ethnic minority groups generally. For example, at one meeting someone suggested Asians with large families would be likely to steal things. Naturally, I challenged this, but no one supported me. That was one of the major problems, I felt totally alone and isolated with no one (especially another black woman) to turn to – particularly in regards to fighting continual racism – which became more and more directed towards me. As far as my performance went, I felt as a black woman I shouldn't ask

Portions of this chapter originally published by M. Davidson in *Psychology at Work* (1996) by P. Warr (ed), London: Penguin.

for help and advice, as it was made clear to me that black women were seen as inferior and lowering the management standards and I didn't want to do anything to reinforce this fallacy. I even worked longer hours than most of the other people there. Towards the end though, I didn't care how black women were perceived – I'd run out of energy and given up. I was not accepted because I was black and female – it was a lose–lose situation. The more assertive I became, the more difficult they (management) made my life. The racism I encountered led to me losing self-esteem and confidence and eventually became depressed and mildly paranoid. I'm now looking for a job in a big city where there are other black people in the organisation.

Over the past 17 years, the author has interviewed and questionnaire surveyed hundreds of female managers as part of numerous different research projects, investigating the experiences of these women's existence in male dominated organisational cultures. Undoubtedly, the majority of these interviewees have been white. However, very occasionally one would, by chance, interview a woman manager from an ethnic minority background and, like the case of Colette above, she would have a very different kind of story to tell.

It is important to note that there are currently differing opinions and inconsistencies regarding descriptive terminology used when describing 'non-white' women and men. In the USA for example, while Asian, Indian, Hispanic, Native American, and African-American women would be referred to collectively as 'women of color', only the African-American group is referred to as 'black' (Hite, 1996). A number of prominent British researchers, such as Mirza (1992) and Bhavnani (1994) used the term 'black' to include women from African, Asian and Caribbean ethnic backgrounds, as well as mixed ethnicity backgrounds. Bhavnani explained her rationale for this choice of terminology when she wrote:

> The words black 'race' and ethnicity are often confused in the research litera-
> ture. . . . The overall use of the word 'black' does not mean that the diversity of
> the black communities in Britain is being discounted; cultural and ethnic iden-
> tities are critical for all peoples, black and white, but they can only be under-
> stood in the context of a racialised and gendered society. 'Race' is a social
> constriction, not a biological one, hence the ethnicity, gender and class is
> subject to constant change.

On the other hand, other British researchers such as Deakins *et al.* (1996) who have recently investigated success factors in 'non-white' entrepreneurs, exclusively use the term 'ethnic minority' to include business owners from various ethnic minority groups. Moreover, these authors totally omit the word 'black' from their publications. Therefore, in an attempt to address this dilemma, the term 'black and ethnic minority' is generally used throughout the book. However, the solo term 'black' is used when specifically adopted by an individual researcher or part of a quotation from either a publication or interviewee.

In 1988, the American academic Nkomo wrote a chapter entitled 'Race and Sex: The Forgotten Case of the Black Female Manager'. In it, she raised the issue of the invisibility of African-American women managers as far as American women in management research was concerned:

> Every time I came across a book or article on women in management I would hurriedly scan the book hoping to find some mention or discussion of the unique experience of black women managers. More often than not I found nothing. . . . The overwhelming implication is that the same sex-role constraints operating as boundaries for white female managers influence the experience of black female managers also. To understand the experience of black female managers, one merely extrapolates findings from the women in management research to black female managers.
>
> (Nkomo, 1988)

Later in 1990, while attending an International Women in Management Conference in Canada, the author met and listened to a lecture by the African-American researcher Ella Bell. Clearly, her research at Harvard substantiated previous American literature which concluded that African-American women managers faced a double jeopardy of sexual and racial discrimination, which secured their position at the very bottom of the managerial pyramid. However, despite research by our American colleagues, to date, there are very few British publications specifically investigating the experiences, problems and pressures of black and ethnic minority managers, male or female. Gilkes (1990) explored childhood, educational, occupational and cultural experiences of 25 UK women community workers from various ethnic minority backgrounds in a Northern city by in-depth, tape recorded interviews. She reported that these women frequently referred to their powerlessness, isolation and victimisation stemming from inequality and status degradation, fostered by negative images and stereotypes attached to black women's work (Gilkes, 1990). More recently, Mirza's (1992) five year longitudinal study of 62 young black and ethnic minority women in London, once again high-lighted the wasted potential of both the men and the women. In the words of Mirza (1992): 'Despite the myth of the "black superwoman" busy outstripping her male counterparts, if you are young, female and black in Britain, chances are slim that you will find a job to reflect your academic ability or potential.' Therefore, the author felt that the experiences of British black and ethnic minority female managers should be systemati-cally studied and highlighted, in the hope of starting a process of corporate awareness and change, as well as encouraging further research to be carried out by researchers from different ethnic groups. With financial support from the Sundridge Park Research Foundation, the author decided to spend six months going round the country and, with the help of a female colleague, Caroline Davey, interviewing a cross section of female managers from African, Asian, Afro-Caribbean and mixed ethnic backgrounds. However, neither of the interviewers came from an ethnic minority background. Both were white, middle class and female. Certainly, for some of the interviewees, the ethnic origin of the interviewees was an issue of concern to them:

> I think I should tell you that I've spoken to some of our black women managers concerning your study. While most are in favour of the concept and willing to be interviewed, a number did raise the issue as to why a black woman was not carrying out this research. A few would not agree to be interviewed because of that.

As a consequence, as white interviewers, this issue was always raised during initial contact and at the beginning of each interview session. This enabled interviewees to discuss their feelings about this issue openly and indeed, some women spoken to highlighted some advantages – as illustrated by the following quotation:

> I feel as a black woman talking to a white woman, I actually am much more detailed and graphic when describing my experiences. If you were black, I would tend to assume that some of the problems I have living in a white world were too obvious to even mention to a woman sharing the same ethnic background.

There is a host of literature pertaining to race and ethnicity in research methods (e.g., Stanfield and Dennis, 1993), with heavy emphasis on the ethics relating to the different gender, socio-economic group and ethnic background of the researchers/interviewers and the research subjects/groups.

In her recent book *Black American Women's Writing – A Quilt of Many Colours* (1994), the British academic Lennox Birch suggests how a white women such as herself can identify with African-American women's experiences through the analysis of their voices expressed in their writings:

> The personal struggle of Afro-American women against marginalisation in America, channelled into establishing for themselves a self-definition in which their beauty, strength and individuality is recognised, is not just one of race, but of gender too. In examining racial prejudice black women writers expose the cultural constraints of class, gender and religion with which white women can also identify. White women cannot, as Barbara Smith points out, share the experiential reality of white racism suffered by black women, but by being exposed to a literature expressing that reality, they can move towards an understanding of their own culturally shaped prejudice, confront their own fear of difference, and realise that there is more that joins black and white women than should ever keep them apart.

> (Lennox Birch, 1994)

The American white sociologist, Margaret Anderson has carried out numerous qualitative studies on the lives of African-American women. In her review of the unique methodological problems for members of both minority and majority groups doing research in minority communities, she makes the following conclusions:

> we should develop research practices that acknowledge and take as central the class, race and gender relations in which researchers and research subjects are situated. At the same time, we should question assumptions that the knower is the ultimate authority on the lives of those whom she or he studies. We should not assume that white scholars are unable to generate research with people of colour as research subjects, but we must be aware that to do so, white scholars must work in ways that acknowledge and challenge white privilege and question how such privilege may shape research experiences.
>
> (Anderson, 1993)

Prior to describing the demographic profile of the women managers who took part in this study, this chapter will review the overall position of women in the workforce and women as managers. Each of these sections will then be followed by specific reviews focusing on what is currently known about black and ethnic minority female workers and managers.

What is evident from the Labour Force Surveys and research literature, is that until relatively recently, the position and experiences of black and ethnic minority, women and men, were largely ignored. References to 'female', in fact, assumed 'white' female. If black and ethnic minority women were included in the samples, they became 'invisible' and were absorbed into the predominantly white populations.

WOMEN AND EMPLOYMENT

Today, in most Western countries, organisations recognise that women represent a significant proportion of the labour force. Since the mid 1970s, British employers have responsibilities towards their employees under both common law and statute, including the Equal Pay and Sex Discrimination Acts, Race Relations Act, Employee Protection Acts and Health and Safety Acts (Wilson, 1995). In 1996 women accounted for 44% of the UK workforce (Labour Market Trends, 1996) and this figure will continue to rise until the year 2006 according to recent UK government projections. Similar trends are evident in Australasia, the USA, Canada and throughout Europe (Davidson, 1996). In the European labour market, women now make up 41% of all adults who are in work or looking for work (Plantenga, 1995). Similar patterns emerge in Australia where women account for 42% of the workforce (Still, 1993). Furthermore, these rates are predicted to continue increasing, particularly among younger women. In the UK, for example, about three-quarters of women are expected to be working by the year 2001.

This significant continued rise in employment among women has its roots in a number of developments. These include the expansion of service industries, the increase in part-time employment, changes in life expectancy, in economic circumstances (especially in relation to employment and housing) and in social expectations. In addition, the changing nature of the family means smaller families and households, later marriage, more cohabitation, more extramarital births, more divorce and more and more people living in one-parent families, predominantly headed by women, with dependent children and dependent elderly relatives (7% of UK households, HMSO, 1995).

Over the past twenty years there has been a swing from employment in traditional industries such as manufacturing towards the service sector, an area of employment which is traditionally female and one which offers plenty of flexible employment patterns. Indeed, for several years, the UK government has promoted greater labour market flexibility in relation to flexible hours, job sharing, part-time working, home working and self-employment (Watson, 1994). In 1996, women represented a third of all those working full-time and 82% of those working part-time (Department for Education and Employment, 1997).

Life stages – particularly parenthood, clearly have a much greater influence on women's working lives than on men's. In 1995, 65% of UK mothers with dependent children were economically active compared with 55% in 1984 (Labour Force Survey, 1995). Among people of working age, 63% of mothers worked part time and the greatest increase in labour market participation has been among women with children aged under four, an increase from 37% in 1984 to 54% in 1996. In contrast, employment grew more slowly or even declined among mothers with no educational background, lone mothers, mothers with a youngest child of secondary school age, mothers with three or more children and black mothers (Sly, 1994). Indeed, it should be noted that despite having higher levels of education and qualifications than white women, in 1996, 16% of ethnic minority women were unemployed. This compares with an official 1996 unemployment rate for white women of 6% and 9% for white men compared to 20% of ethnic minority men.

Recent evidence in the UK suggests that at school, girls are attaining better academic examination results compared to boys. The 1995 National Consortium for Examination Results showed that girls were almost ten points ahead of boys for the third year running at GCSE level. In 1995, girls and boys were level in subjects such as maths and science with girls excelling in language based subjects – this, despite the set-back of continuous assessment of course work which was suggested by some to favour girls over boys.

Not surprisingly, there have also been significant increases in the number of females going into higher education. From 1995/96, while at the post-graduate level, men's enrolments still outnumber women's, at the undergraduate level there are now more women students. There are also increasing trends for women graduates to move into areas of managerial and professional employment which were previously dominated by men. In 1973, only 10% of students studying for social administration and business degrees were women, whereas today in the UK more than 45% of these students are female (Davidson and Cooper, 1992). A recent survey of ten UK companies who kept detailed records of their graduate intake over the last ten years found that Shell had tripled the number of women graduates it recruits, while Unilever had more than doubled its intake. Other companies such as National Westminster Bank, Barclays, ICL, Coopers and Lybrand and Abbey National, had also seen big increases in the number of graduate women they recruit (Webber, 1994).

Nevertheless, occupational segregation by gender still persists in all European labour markets. More than 50% of employed women are found in service or clerical jobs, compared with 20% of men (Plantenga, 1995). According to Rubery and Fagan (1993), the majority of the new jobs women moved into in the 1980s were in two occupational areas: professional jobs and clerical jobs. Therefore, while an increasing number of women are entering the lower level service and clerical jobs which are already female dominated; some women are gaining access to highly skilled professional jobs, including management.

Similar trends are recurring in Australasia and the USA. In Australia, 55% of female employees in 1992 were concentrated in two major occupational groups: clerks and sales persons. While 20% of Australian female employees were in professional and para-professional occupations, 22% were registered nurses (Australian Bureau of Statistics, 1992). Even in the USA, with the strongest legislation affecting the employment of women, women are most frequently found in the helping professions, and sales and retail jobs. In 1992, US women held 98% of secretarial, typist and stenographer positions, 79% of administrative jobs, and 94% of registered nurse positions (US Department of Labor, 1992).

There have, however, been some advances in women entering traditionally male dominated jobs and in all the European Union countries, women are increasing their share of professional jobs. In the UK, for example, women now account for 54% of newly qualified solicitors, which is an increase of nearly 9% over the last 7 years. There has also been an increase by 10% of women becoming chartered accountants over the past 10 years and they now account for 37% of newly qualified accountants (Wilkinson, 1994). Even so, the majority of women in professional jobs are still concentrated in the caring professions and the public sector and are occupying the lower managerial positions (Davidson and Burke, 1994). Even in those industries in which women predominate, they tend to have the less prestigious jobs. For example, only 3 in 10 secondary school head and deputy head teachers are women, even though half of secondary school teachers are female (HMSO, 1995).

While the evidence suggests that it is relatively easy for women to gain employment at the lower levels of organisations, it is still proving very difficult for them to reach upper middle and senior management positions and the percentage of senior female executives is very small. In Britain, there are approximately three million managers with about a fifth being women; of the million or so middle and senior managers, at most 4% are women (Davidson and Cooper, 1992; Davidson and Burke, 1994).

BLACK AND ETHNIC MINORITY WOMEN AND EMPLOYMENT

To date, the most comprehensive analysis of the position of black and ethnic minority women in the UK Labour Force has been carried out by Bhavnani (1994). Due to the increasing incidences of racial discrimination, several Race Relations Acts have been passed, the most recent being the 1976 Race Relations Act. In addition, The Commission for Racial Equality was set up.

Bhavnani (1994) adopts the word 'black' in her reference to women from African, Asian and Caribbean ethnic backgrounds. She recounts how the presence of 'black' people in Britain can be traced back to Roman times. In order to service the needs of the aristocracy, the introduction of slavery was a highly profitable trading economy. Hence, these women have had links with Britain for thousands of years. However, it was not until the beginning of the 1950s, 1960s, to the 1970s, that most black and ethnic minority women arrived in Britain. Bhavnani (1994) asserts that this affected their position in the labour market. Hindu, Afro-Caribbean and Sikh women arrived early in the migration phase at a time of stability and economic growth. Bangladeshi and Pakistani women on the other hand, tended to arrive in the 1970s in order to join their male relatives, already in Britain.

Bhavnani (1994) points out that it is only since 1984 that the collection of large scale survey data on 'black' women in the labour market commenced. In Britain, around 5% of the population of working age are of African, Afro-Caribbean or Asian origin. Indications are that this proportion is likely to grow in the coming years and more black and ethnic minority employees are entering managerial positions (Iles and Auluck, 1991). In 1995 around 71% of British women aged 16–59 were economically active. For black and ethnic minority women, the average economic activity rate was 57.6%. More specifically, 76% of Afro-Caribbean women were economically active compared to 61% of Indian women, 29% of Pakistani women and 22% of Bangladeshi women (Bhavnani, 1994). This compares to a rate of 71.4% for white women. However, while 56.3% of white women worked full-time, 69.8% of black and ethnic minority women were full-time workers. Bhavnani (1994) suggests reasons for this are material as well as due to demands from certain industries. They are more and more likely to work on a casual/temporary basis in jobs previously done by white women, and are also likely to be working as home workers in certain industrial sections, often hidden from official statistics.

Of the 3 million black and ethnic minority people in Britain, most are concentrated in the metropolitan areas and work in the urban markets. The

Table 1.1   Employment by industry and ethnic origin, 1989–1991 (%)

	Men		Women	
	White	Ethnic minority groups	White	Ethnic minority groups
Agriculture, forestry, fishing	3	–	1	–
Energy and water supply	3	–	1	–
Extraction of minerals, metal manufacture etc.	4	3	2	–
Metal goods, engineering and vehicles	14	13	5	6
Other manufacturing of which:	10	11	8	11
Footwear, clothing and leather goods	1	2	2	5
Construction	13	5	2	–
Distribution, hotels, catering and repairs of which:	16	30	25	24
Wholesale distribution	4	3	3	3
Retail distribution	8	15	15	15
Hotels and catering	2	9	7	7
Transport and communications of which:	8	11	3	5
Postal services and communications	2	4	1	–
Banking and finance etc. of which:	10	10	13	12
Business services	6	6	6	6
Other services of which:	18	17	41	40
Public administration, national defence etc.	6	4	6	6
Education	4	3	11	6
Medical/health/veterinary services	2	5	9	15
Other services to the public	2	3	11	10
All industries: overall nos (000s)	13276	580	10600	393

Source: Labour Force Surveys 1989–1991. House of Commons Hansard, 21 May 1992, cols 249-50 (Amin and Oppeneim, 1992:10).
Notes: These figures exclude those on government employment and training schemes.
    The – indicates less than 10,000 in sample: estimate not shown.
    The totals include those who did not specify industry.
    'Other public services' comprises all other public services excluding sanitary, research and development, recreational and domestic services.
    Percentages do not all add up to 100% because of rounding.
Source: Bhavnani (1994) p. 72.

highest percentage (21.4%) of ethnic minority women of working age live in Greater London with the lowest numbers (7%) living in Berkshire and West Yorkshire (Owen, 1994).

Table 1.1 illustrates the industry distribution by all groups and gender. Bhavnani (1994) notes that this table highlights that there is a greater disparity between white and 'black' men than between women overall:

> Black people as a whole are likely to be over represented in particular industrial sectors by ethnicity, so for example, African-Asians, Indians and Pakistanis are over represented in the retail distribution sector, Chinese in hotels and catering. Pakistanis in transport and communications and Afro-Caribbeans and Africans in health care and other services.
>
> (Bhavnani, 1994)

Nevertheless, she emphasises that 'black' women do experience differing patterns of segregation in the labour market, compared to white women, 'black' men and white men. In the words of Bhavnani (1994):

> Horizontal and vertical segregation are both racialised and gendered. For example, it is primarily black women who work in ancillary occupations in the health service; in hotel and catering black women are to be found primarily in low paid manual work, with a much greater degree of concentration than white women. Black women are occupationally segregated. For example, black nurses are concentrated in work with the elderly and in mental health. . . . Some women of South Asian origin are concentrated in the food and textile industries; Afro-Caribbean women work in the least desirable sectors of the health service, Chinese and Bangladeshi women overwhelmingly work in the restaurant trade. Pakistani, Gujarati and Bangladeshi women are also more likely to engage in home working.

WOMEN IN BUSINESS AND MANAGEMENT

In the European Union countries, fewer than 5% of women are in senior management roles. However, there is an increasing trend for women to start their own businesses with between 15% and 30% of entrepreneurs or business owners in the European Union being female (Davidson and Cooper, 1993). In the USA women-owned small businesses have increased from 5% in 1970 to 33% in 1996 (*The Economist*, 1996a) with forecasts of the figure reaching 50% by the year 2000 (Tarr Whelan, 1994). In the UK, with nearly a quarter of all self-employed being women this is a figure which has doubled since 1980 (Department for Education and Employment, 1996). While many of these businesses are small, they are undoubtedly growing in size and number. In the US for example, the number of employees in women-owned businesses that have 100 or more workers is rising more than twice as fast as average for all such American firms (*The Economist*, 1996b). Indeed, it has been suggested that the control and flexibility provided by owning one's own business, are often a greater attraction to working women, particularly those with children, than is employment in a hierarchy-driven, male-dominated corporate culture (Marshall, 1994, 1995).

Women are still most likely to be managers in those occupations which are traditionally female, such as catering and retail. While the majority of both male and female managers were concentrated in the private and service sectors, women were found less in manufacturing than men and were employed more in service organisations, such as professional services, education, training and government. Women are also more likely to be found in certain managerial occupations, such as personnel, office administration and training, and in organisations where there is a higher than

Table 1.2   Females – sample size by responsibility level (%)

	1974	1983	1991	1993	1994	1995	1996
Directors	0.6	0.3	2.6	2.8	2.8	3.0	3.3
Functions heads	0.4	1.5	6.1	6.8	6.1	5.8	6.5
Department heads	2.1	1.9	8.1	9.0	8.7	9.7	12.2
Section leader	2.4	5.3	11.6	13.2	12.0	14.2	14.4
Whole sample	1.8	3.3	8.6	10.2	9.5	10.7	12.3

Source: Institute of Management and Remuneration Economics (1996)

average number of women. However, even in those professions where women constitute a high percentage of the workforce, such as teaching and personnel, men still dominate the senior positions (Vinnicombe and Colwill, 1995). For example, while 44% of personnel managers were female in 1994, only 9.5% of personnel directors were women (Lownes, 1994).

In Australia, Governmental Affirmative Action Policy has resulted in an increase of women in management over the past decade and they now constitute 25% of all managers. However, Australian women managers are still concentrated in the junior ranks and Hede (1995) predicts that if recent trends continue, Australian women will not reach 50% of the managerial category for well over 70 years.

In the USA, with the strongest legislation in the form of Affirmative Action Policies affecting the employment of women, this type of gender segregation in management appears to be breaking down at a more rapid rate. The ranks of female managers tripled during the 1970s and, by 1979 30.5% of American managers were women. In 1996, this figure has risen to over 48%. However, despite legislation, American female workers are still finding the 'glass ceiling' – the invisible but very real career progression barriers – difficult to 'shatter' at senior executive level, where women constitute around 5% of managerial positions. This percentage has hardly changed in the last decade (*The Economist*, 1996b).

Nevertheless, there have been increasing numbers of women entering various management levels in British organisations over the past two decades. Table 1.2 illustrates the number of female managers at different levels in the UK's largest organisations since 1974. The figures were compiled by the UK National Management Survey carried out by the Institute of Management and Remuneration Economics, and show that with the exception of 1994, the percentage of women managers has gradually risen to 12.3% in 1996.

The 1996 survey also confirmed that the average profile of the female manager compared to her male counterpart has hardly changed over the past decade. She earns less, even at Director level, and on average females are six to eight years younger at each responsibility level with the average female manager being 37 years old compared to 44 for male managers. Still, the most popular jobs for women managers are personnel and marketing, in both of which females make up around 35% of managers. The least popular jobs are in physical distribution, research and development, purchasing and contracting and manufacturing and production, where fewer than 6% of managers are women.

THE BLACK AND ETHNIC MINORITY WOMAN MANAGER

Numerous cross-cultural studies have concluded that white managerial women experience unique sources of stress related to their minority status and gender and that these pressures result in higher levels of overall occupational stress compared to their male counterparts (Greenglass, 1985; Devanna, 1987; Davidson and Cooper, 1982, 1983, 1987, 1992; Davidson, 1996). Overall, research findings indicate that white women managers experience more external discriminatory based pressures including strains of coping with discrimination, prejudice and sex stereotyping; lack of role models and feelings of isolation; burdens of coping with the role of 'token woman'; and higher work/home conflict pressures (Davidson and Cooper, 1992; Davidson *et al.*, 1995).

Furthermore, American research confirms that African-American and other ethnic minority managers, particularly women, are *doubly disadvantaged* in terms of upward mobility and high levels of work and home pressures (Bell, 1990; Greenhaus *et al.*, 1990; Dickens and Dickens, 1991; Hite, 1996). Indeed, according to Isles and Auluck (1991) 'Such findings in American studies of black managers resemble those often reported for white women managers in Britain'. In the USA, the number of African-American employees occupying managerial positions has increased from 3.6% of the national total in 1977 to 5.2% in 1982, to 6% of all managers in 1986 (Greenhaus *et al.*, 1990). In 1988, 72% of all managers in American companies employing more than 100 people were white men, 23% white women, 3% African-American men and 2% African-American women (Reskin and Padovic, 1994). In 1994, according to the US Bureau of Labor Statistics, in the category of executive, administrative, and managerial occupations, white women hold 38% of the positions, while women 'of color' represent only 5% (Hite, 1996).

According to the most recent 1988–90 (British) Labour Force Survey, 9% of ethnic minority females in the UK are found in the category – 'Professional Manager, Employer, Employees and Managers – large establishments', compared to 11% of white females. It should be noted, however, that the high percentage of ethnic women in the 'professional' category may be misleading since this also includes nursing (see Table 1.3). While there has been a small overall rise in ethnic minority women in higher grade employment, these women continue to be under-represented in this category compared to white women (Bhavnani, 1994). For example, of the general managerial and

Table 1.3 Job levels of female employees by ethnic group, 1988–1990 (%)

	All Origins	White	Total Ethnic Minority	Afro-Caribbean	African Asian	Indian	Pakistani	Bangladeshi	Chinese	African	Other/Mixed
Prof/manager/employer	11	11	9	8	7	10	4	*	16	11	12
Employees and managers – large establishments	6	6	4	5	3	4	1	*	4	5	4
Employees and managers – small establishments	4	4	3	2	2	2	3	*	5	3	4
Professional workers – employees	2	2	2	1	2	4	0	*	7	2	3
Other non-manual	55	56	53	54	58	47	42	*	53	47	63
Skilled manual and foremen	5	5	5	4	9	5	7	*	2	6	3
Semi-skilled manual	22	22	27	25	25	34	45	*	20	32	17
Unskilled manual	7	7	5	9	1	4	2	*	9	4	5
Armed services/inadequately described/not stated	0	0	0	0	0	0	0	*	0	1	0

* Sample size too small

Source: 1988–1990 Labour Force Surveys (Jones, 1993: Table 4.11)

administrators' jobs held by women in 'national/local government, large companies and organisations' in the UK in 1991, 1.4% were filled by Afro-Caribbean women. Moreover, only 1.3% of women in 'other managers and administrators' category were Afro-Caribbean, 0.7% of women who were 'specialist managers' and 'managers in transport and storing', and 0.6% of women who were 'financial institutions and office managers, and civil service executive officers' (African and Caribbean Finance Forum *et al.*, 1996).

Very little is known about the numbers of ethnic minority female entrepreneurs. Between 1979 and 1984 ethnic minority female small business owners constituted 5.7% of all female business owners. Furthermore, between 1987 and 1989 more than 34,000 ethnic minority women in the UK were self-employed of which 12,000 had employees (Bakshi, 1992; Bhavnani, 1994). This compares to 5.2% of all male small business owners being made up of ethnic minority males. Moreover, some minority communities such as Chinese, Cypriots and South Asians have secured significant presence in certain local economies and sectors. Asians, for example, are reputed to control over half of Britain's retail trade (Aziz, 1995). According to Ram and Barr (1996) the assistance of business support agencies has facilitated this prominence:

> Encouraging ethnic minority communities into business has been an implicit feature of the small firm policy agenda since the 1980s. Developments like the creation of the Ethnic Minority Business Initiative in 1985, the emergence of black-led Enterprise Agencies, and the staging of a national Business Link conference on ethnic enterprise in March 1996 suggests continuing policy interest.

To date, research addressing the issues of black and ethnic minority managers has been almost exclusively American (predominantly black African-Americans) and the amount of total published research is according to a review by Cox and Nkomo (1990): 'Small, relative to the importance of the topic'. Indeed, Bell (1990), Bell *et al.* (1993) and Betters-Reed and Moore (1995) emphasised that studies of African-American and professional 'women of color', especially in corporate settings, are virtually excluded from the growing body of research on women in management. The assumption has been, 'women in management' refers to 'white' women in management.

Nevertheless, from the limited research studies available, what is clear is that ethnic minority managers tend to be under-represented in the majority of American and British organisations, particularly at middle and higher managerial levels of the organisational hierarchy, and for them, the glass ceiling is even harder to shatter (Greenhaus *et al.*, 1990; Iles and Auluck, 1991). In her study of the development of 'black' nurses in the NHS, Mayor (1996) suggests that black men and women experience a series of 'cold spots', or smoked glass ceilings in their career progress. She concludes that the threshold of the glass ceiling for black professionals is set lower than the level experienced by white women managers. In another recent British report addressing the position of Afro-Caribbean people in management, the glass ceiling concept is transformed into 'the cement roof' (African and Caribbean Finance Forum *et al.*, 1996).

Bell (1990) was one of the first researchers to have carried out studies specifically investigating the experiences and problems faced by ethnic minority women managers and professionals in America. Her studies reveal that African-American women perceive themselves as living in a bicultural world (one culture black, the other white). Consequently, the women feel a constant 'push and pull' between the different cultural contexts in their lives, which results in high stress levels particularly linked to role conflict stressors. Denton's review (1990) also emphasises the importance of these bicultural role stressors and the combined effects of *racism and sexism* which enhance the 'stresses endemic to today's cadre of black professional women'. Furthermore, compared to their white female counterparts, these women managers are more likely to be in token and test-case positions (Bell *et al.*, 1993). Due to the scarcity of research in this area, particularly in the UK, Bhavnani (1994) stated:

> We also need to ask some questions about black women in management. Is the rate of entry into management slower than for white women? How are junior and middle management positions changing? How do these changes affect the conditions and job responsibilities of black women managers?

ISSUES INVESTIGATED

The aim of this book is to investigate the problems, pressures and barriers faced by black and ethnic minority British female managers in the 1990s. The term black and ethnic minority is used to include women from African, Asian, Caribbean and mixed ethnic backgrounds. The interview sample aimed to constitute a cross section of black and ethnic minority women managers working in a variety of managerial levels, management jobs, organisations and industries, in both public and private sectors, throughout the UK (see Tables 1.4, 1.5 and 1.6). The majority of the sample worked in large organisations (66.7%), a third worked in the private sector and half of the organisations had predominantly female employees. With the exception of a few very small organisations which had predominantly ethnic minority employees, the remainder of the interviewees worked in organisations where ethnic minority workers constituted a very low percentage of the total workforce (see Table 1.5).

Table 1.6 illustrates that 46.7% of the sample were Afro-Caribbean, 23.3% were Indian, 10% Pakistani, 6.7% African and 13.3% of mixed white/black ethnic origin. Bangladeshi women were not included as to date, the percentage who are managers is too small a sample size to be included in

Table 1.4 Black and ethnic minority female managers interview sample (N = 30)

Industrial sectors	Occupational title	
	Public sector	Private sector
Civil Service	Deputy Head – Race Relations Unit	Market Research Manager
County Councils	Policy Development Manager	Self-Employed Education Consultant
Voluntary Sector	Asian Community Worker/ Education	Production Plant Manager
Prison/Probationary Service	Senior Equality Officer	Head of Flight Operations
Health Service	Fieldwork Team Manager	Finance Manager
Education Sector	Associate Director – Service Development	Commissioning Editor
Retail Sector	Residential Manager in Probation Service	Personnel Manager
Publishing	Homeless Manager	Information Technology Manager
Finance Sector	National Children's Officer	Equal Opportunities Manager
Aviation	Commissioner Project Manager	Business Advisor to Black/Ethnic Minorities
Pharmaceutical Sector	Consumer Affairs Director	
Telecommunications Sector	Director/Senior Executive – Health Information Director Head of Midwifery/Gynaecology Personnel Manager Chief Nursing Consultant Senior Training Officer Administrative Officer Careers Advisor Councillor	

Labour Force Surveys. Their ages ranged from 26 to 51 years, with a mean age of 36. One third of the sample were in senior management positions, 43% in middle management and 23% occupied junior management positions. The average salary was £26,500 per annum, 83% worked full-time and 87% had had continuous work patterns. Seventy per cent of the sample were married or in a partnership with 7% having been divorced. It should be noted that compared to their white female counterparts, Asian female managers, in particular, are more likely to be married – often arranged marriages – and much less likely to be divorced. Consequently, this was a sample of professional, successful, middle-class black and ethnic minority women managers.

CONCLUSIONS

This book endeavours to share the stories and experiences of the 30 black and ethnic minority women managers interviewed as part of the study. The

Table 1.5 Employment

	%	(N)
Organisational profile		
Large	66.7	(20)
Medium	13.3	(4)
Small	20.0	(6)
Public	66.7	(20)
Private	33.3	(10)
Predominantly female employees	50.0	(15)
Predominantly male employees	30.0	(9)
Approximately equal female and male employees	20.0	(6)
Percentage of ethnic minority workers in organisation		
Less than 2%	43.3	(13)
Less than 5%	16.7	(5)
Less than 10%	13.3	(4)
Less than 20%	13.3	(4)*
Less than 50%	3.3	(1)*
90%-100%	10.0	(3)*
Prominent ethnic background of other co-workers		
White males	16.7	(5)
White males and females	30.0	(9)
White females	13.3	(4)
White and black/ethnic minority males	3.3	(1)
White and black/ethnic minority males and females	16.7	(5)
White and black/ethnic minority females	6.7	(2)
Black/ethnic minority males	0.0	(0)
Black/ethnic minority males and females	6.7	(2)
Black/ethnic minority females	6.7	(2)

* Very small organisations

majority spoke openly and honestly about their past and present lives, as well as about their hopes and dreams for the future and their children's future. Firstly, childhood and past and current home experiences are recounted in the following chapter. Here, the double negative effects of sexism and racism are introduced and both these issues continue to be important negative themes throughout the book. Next, role conflicts inherent in living in a bicultural world – one black, one white – both at work and at home are revealed in Chapter 3. The next three chapters concentrate on the work environment – the racial taboos and negative stereotypes linked to relationships at work; causes and symptoms of occupational stress and the issues involved in acquiring appropriate management skills; and finally, the effects of racism and sexism on career development. The last chapter presents a model to summarise a typical profile and major barriers/pressures at work, home and socially, faced by the black and ethnic minority female manager, along with the negative outcomes in terms of stress and career development. This final chapter will focus on what individuals, organisa-

Table 1.6   Profile of Black and Ethnic Minority Female Manager (N = 30)

	%	(N)
Age		
Mean age, 35.8 years (range 26–51 years)		
Ethnic Background		
Afro-Caribbean	46.7	(14)
Indian	23.3	(7)
Pakistani	10.0	(3)
African	6.7	(2)
Other	13.3	(4)
Birth Place		
UK born	43.3	(13)
Non UK born	56.7	(17)
(Mean years in UK 24.6 years – range 10–38 years)		
Marital Status		
Married/living with someone	70.0	(21)
Single	30.0	(9)
(Of those single 44.4% (N = 4) single parents and 6.7% of total sample divorced)		
Children/Dependants		
Total sample with children	60.0	(18)
Those with other dependants at home	10.0	(3)
		(Range 1–4 children)
Type of Employment		
Full-time	83.0	(25)
Part-time	10.0	(3)
Job share	6.7	(2)
Salary		
Mean salary per annum	£26,500	(Range £11–50,000)
Employment History		
Mean years in lifetime of employment	13.4 years	(Range 4–33 years)
Mean years in present job	2.9 years	(Range 4–35 years)
Percentage with continuous career pattern	86.7	
Management Level		
Senior	33.3	(10)
Middle	43.3	(13)
Junior	23.3	(7)

tions, governments and unions can do to help ensure equality of opportunity for these female managers, as well as emphasise the need for changes in behaviour and attitudes. What is clear, is that compared to their white managerial female counterparts, rather than a 'glass ceiling', black and ethnic minority women managers are much more likely to encounter a ceiling made of *concrete*.

All of the interviewees wholeheartedly supported the research and wanted to be informed of future publications. Many also wanted to set up a network group of interviewees and this has already been achieved. This book attempts to present these women's experiences as honestly and as objectively as the author felt able, and hopefully has gone some way to achieve the goals outlined by Anderson (1993) when she wrote:

> As whites learn to see the world through the experiences of others, a process that is itself antithetical to the views of privileged groups, we can begin to construct more complete and less disturbed ways of seeing the complex relations of race, chaos and gender

2

Past and Present Home Environments

Racism was always a factor for me during my education.
You were ostracised quietly – a kind of subversive bullying.
It actually pushed me academically as I was determined to
prove them wrong.

Two of the leading American researchers in African-American female managers, Ella Bell and Stella Nkomo, advocate a holistic approach to studying women managers which incorporates core elements of gender, race, ethnicity, and class as well as the role of history. In particular, they emphasise the importance of recording the story of women's lives:

> The story begins with her earliest recollections of childhood and continues through time, each experience building on the achievements, disappointments, struggles, celebrations, and relationships from past events. What a woman comes to understand about the world, her sense of self-worth, her skill level, and the quality of life she comes to expect – all originate early in life.
>
> (Bell and Nkomo, 1992)

Developmental psychologists tend to view young children as often being malleable and growing up in a complex social world which they commonly adapt to. Thus, experiences with mothers, fathers, surrogates, siblings and peers, the quality of child-care and schooling and ethnic, cultural, racial and socio-economic factors, can all affect development. In this chapter, the stories of the interviewees' childhood and adolescent experiences, parental relationships, and current home situations, are revealed.

CHILDHOOD AND FAMILY EXPERIENCES

Naturally, the women we spoke to had different childhood and family experiences which were also determined by their ethnic origin, place of birth, socio-economic background, family dynamics, and parent–child relationships.

Just under half (13) of our interviewees had been born in the UK, almost all of their mothers had worked, full or part-time, and just over half held professional jobs. Almost 60% of their fathers held professional jobs either in the UK or formerly in their homeland, having to sometimes take manual jobs after moving to the UK. For those women who had been born in Britain, most of their parents had joined the British labour market in the boom years from 1945 until the late 1960s. Many of the women we spoke to conceded that whilst growing up, they were subjected to certain degrees of sex-role stereotyping by their parents e.g. having to help more in the house or being expected to cook whilst their brothers weren't. However, the majority recalled that either one or both parents instilled in them high achievement needs, particularly if they were first born. One Pakistani senior executive said: 'As the eldest, I was expected to show the way for my brothers. I can never remember being treated any differently by my parents. If anything, I think they pushed me more than the boys.' Interestingly, nearly half (14) of the sample were first born or only children. This very much parallels the recent study of 48 successful British white women who had achieved extraordinary levels of career success (White, Cox and Cooper, 1992). Fifty four percent of White *et al.*'s women were first-born and numerous other studies have highlighted the performance of first-born children among high achievers (e.g. Auster and Auster, 1981; Hisrich and Brush, 1987). Developmental psychologists propose that factors such as sole parental attention and pressure to achieve help enhance self-confidence and ambition in first-borns (Kagan and Moss, 1962).

The majority of the Afro-Caribbean women emphasised the important dominant role played by women in their culture and the importance of a strong maternal role-model:

> Although I was taught to cook (unlike my brother), I was brought up experiencing Afro-Caribbean women as high achievers. It was instilled in me from an early age that that was one way we could better ourselves. The strength and driving power of my mother acted as a significant role model.

Mirza (1992) also highlighted the strong role model of the mother figure in West Indian families. She found that the young Afro-Caribbean women in her study all described an ideology stressing the relative autonomy of both the female and the male roles.

Parental Expectations – Education and Career

Both American and British research has emphasised the importance of education in ethnic minority families as a means of scaling the class ladder (Simpson, 1984; Higginbotham and Weber, 1992; Mirza, 1992). Simpson's (1984) study of African-American female lawyers revealed that almost all had had parents who had impressed on them as children the importance of education. This was also evident in the women we spoke to with 87% maintaining that their parents instilled in them the importance of education and setting their goals on a career. Similar to Epstein's (1973) interviews with 31 African-American professional women over twenty years ago, most of the women appeared to originate from families which stressed middle-class values, whether or not their incomes permitted middle-class amenities. A number of the Afro-Caribbean women managers described their historical cultural emphasis on education, particularly for girls: 'In Jamaica – the notion was that if you're not educated, then nothing will happen for you. In fact education was certainly more important for girls as they often would leave home earlier.' A senior female executive from Pakistan always remembered the following words said to her by her father: 'No one can take away your knowledge, other things, yes, but knowledge will remain with you always. Those were very significant words for me as my parents had lost all their wealth.'

Mirza (1992) believes that the evidence for the success of 'black' young people in British education is often ignored. Numerous studies have shown that due to greater motivation and parental encouragement, black and ethnic minority young people are more likely to stay on to further education than white (Bhavnani, 1994). Moreover, young Afro-Caribbean women are more likely to continue their education after leaving school compared to white women, Afro-Caribbean men and white men (Jones, 1993). 'Black' students, particularly 'black' female students, have lower university acceptance rates than white (Bhavnani, 1994). However, indications are that younger black and ethnic minority women are receiving more qualifications in higher education institutions. Compared to 13% of white women, 15% of West Indian/Guyanese and 20% of other ethnic minority groups (Chinese, Africans, Indians) have qualifications. This compares to the figure for Bangladeshis and Pakistanis of 9% (Bhavnani, 1994).

Table 2.1 shows that the sample female managers were highly educated with two thirds having gained degrees at undergraduate and postgraduate level. In addition, 25 out of the 30 had also gained additional professional qualifications. Consequently, this group of women managers were *even more highly* educated than White *et al.*'s (1992) sample of high-flying white women. About half had a degree, compared to 6% of women in general, which meant they were slightly better qualified than white male chief executives studied by Cox and Cooper (1988) and White *et al.* (1992). However, despite their educational achievements, many of the interviewees remembered personal incidences of racism, particularly those who attended school

Table 2.1   Highest educational level of sample managers (N = 30)

Highest educational level	%	(N)
GCSEs (O levels)	3.3	(1)
A levels	23.3	(7)
Diploma	6.7	(2)
Degree	33.3	(10)
Postgraduate degree	33.3	(10)
Additional professional qualifications	83.3	(25)

in Britain and found themselves in a situation where there were very few (if any) students from the same ethnic background:

> In school, you always felt like a second class citizen and this was more due to my colour but also due to my gender. You had to learn to defend yourself.

> I went to an all girls school and because I came near the top in my class, I was picked on by the white girls and called 'a black swot'. I was very sensitive and found life very difficult. I'd get pushed about and bullied and one day I physically lashed out – that seemed to stop it.

Bhavnani (1994) emphasises the importance of the framework of how racism has developed and been *integral* to the formation of British society rather than an *external* problem. For her, race and racism is linked to the development of class and gender divisions within British society rather than the arrival of 'black immigrants' after World War II. Bhavnani views 'race' and racism as a social construction constantly changing:

> 'Race' and racism are economical, political, ideological and social constructions. They are not fixed but changing phenomena. Understanding 'race' and racism as shifting dynamic concepts has inevitable implications for analysis; racism is not the 'same' everywhere, rather it changes according to the nature of the wider context. There are, therefore, different racisms which impact on differing groups differently. This does not mean there is a hierarchy of racisms; rather the logic of this proposition suggests analysis according to specificity of experience.

American research suggests that no matter when black and ethnic minority people first encounter a predominantly white or integrated setting, it is always a shock. According to Higginbotham and Weber (1992): 'The experience of racial exclusion cannot prepare people of colour to deal with the racism in daily face-to-face encounters with white people.'

For many of the women who experienced this type of racist bullying at school, it often made them more determined to succeed: 'Racism was always a factor for me during my education. You were ostracised quietly – a kind of subversive bullying. It actually pushed me academically as I was determined to prove them wrong.' Not only did some of the women complain of being steered away from science subjects, like their white female counterparts, whilst at school, but they also felt that they suffered racial stereotyping and sometimes their achievements were undermined. For example, one Asian middle manager recalled: 'At junior school, the children would make racist remarks and I also noticed racism from staff. I was expected, for instance, to be good at sport because I was tall and black. At college, when I did well at the secretarial exam, my tutors accused me of cheating!' Another woman remembers her last year at junior school having moved to the UK from Barbados at the age of 10: 'I was an excellent student, always did my homework religiously and I was particularly good at maths. Then one day my maths teacher sent home a note for my father saying that he mustn't do my maths homework for me anymore!' Mirza's (1992) study of young British black and ethnic minority women found evidence of overt and intentional racism by white teachers towards black female students. However, while these young women often continued to display positive self-esteem and often challenged their teachers expectations of them – 'they were in no position in the "power hierarchy" to counteract any negative outcomes of these interpretations' (Mirza, 1992).

Certainly, the experiences of some of these women managers reinforced Bhavnani's (1994) conclusion that: 'Young black women suffer the complex impact of "race" and gender stereotyping in education, yet they continue to view education as a primary means of changing stereotypical expectations.' However, in addition to almost all the interviewees' parents showing positive and encouraging attitudes to towards their daughters' education, all but four of the women said that one or both parent emphasised the importance of a career (rather than a 'job'). An Afro-Caribbean director described her father's words to her, a week before he died: 'As far as possible, ensure you work for yourself and even if you don't – *act* as if you do.' While many of the interviewees' parents did not stress a specific occupation *per se* 'which they wanted their daughters to pursue, popular professions which were mentioned included the caring professions teaching, accounting, law and medicine. It is interesting to note that White *et al.* (1992) concluded that the parents of their high-flying white women, who were ambitious for their daughters to succeed without pressurising them to follow a prescribed direction, facilitated conscious decision-making. Certainly this seems to have been the case for many of the women managers interviewed.

Parental Expectations – Marriage

Although education and the pursuit of a career appear to be common ambitions of parents of both successful white and black and ethnic minority women managers, unlike their white counterparts, these women managers are much more likely to experience parental pressure to marry. Just under half (13) of our sample recalled that their parents emphasised marriage and children as a primary life goal for them, particularly after they had completed their education or in some cases, as they got older.

This type of parental pressure was almost equally split between both Afro-Caribbean and Asian women managers, although the latter were likely to be subjected to arranged marriage, a practice which involves parents choosing 'suitable' prospective marriage partners who are introduced to their daughters. She then has the choice to accept or not. Almost all the Asian women, who had followed this culturally traditional route, appeared content. One very senior executive Pakistani woman recalled: 'I was perfectly happy to be married at 16. My parents introduced me to my husband and the chemistry took place between us straight away. We've now been married 32 years.' Another Indian project manager in her mid-twenties described her experience: 'After I'd finished my education my parents said "right – you're going to get married". They found me a partner – they were happy – I was happy.' However, for one Indian woman in her mid-thirties, who had 'rebelled' and chosen her own marriage partner, the subsequent strain in her relationship with her parents had been immense:

My mum always stressed marriage for me much more than my father who tended to emphasise education. In the end, I married at 19 to someone who was solely my choice. They weren't at all happy because they hadn't chosen him but in the end, gave in. I felt an awful lot of guilt for not having followed 'the script' set by my parents. I didn't start feeling better until after about four years, once my daughter was born. Moving away from my family helped as they always gave the impression they thought my husband and I would split up. However, I never lost the strong pull of my family, and we moved back again to be near them.

Once interviewees who were single reached their late twenties, many reported that parental pressure to marry intensified. This was even the case for an Indian executive in her forties, now married with two children:

My parents had a very modern approach and encouraged us to leave home and go to university. We were middle-class but my father was disinherited for marrying my mother so we were less well off than we would have been. Career was viewed as being the most important and we were expected to choose our own partners freely. They were however, surprised when I turned down some marriage proposals. Then, when I entered my late twenties, they started to put pressure on me to get married.

Parental Relationships – Crossing the Colour Line

Higginbotham and Weber's (1992) American research coined the phrase 'crossing the colour line'. They highlighted the complexity of mobility for black Americans which involves not only crossing class lines but also crossing cultural and racial ones as well. For some of the sample, the intricacies of this type of mobility propelled ultimately by their education and career success, sometimes affected their parental and family relationships, particularly those involving class background.

A highly successful Afro-Caribbean woman executive described her dilemma:

I do have a problem as my parents now view me as slightly above them. My mum rings me up and says things like 'you're the brainy one'. I didn't know how to react. I tend to become distant and not talk about my work when I see them. Recently, I didn't send them an article I'd had published – my friend sent it to them and my mother was upset.

An Indian women manager in the public sector claimed: 'I feel that some members of my family are very envious of my success although I don't feel guilty about it. I am accused of having aimed above my station.' A handful of women interviewees also mentioned that they felt family and friends accused them of 'selling out to the white society' as the following two quotations illustrate:

> My daughter is the only black in her class. Now my family call my child 'a little English woman'. When my daughter sees my parents she switches and starts talking 'the lingo' – she also mixes well with the white society. It's very difficult.

> Some of my black friends were suspicious when I did my degree. I was accused of going into an all-white establishment.

PRESENT HOME SITUATIONS

Literature on white women managers has emphasised the strains of maintaining their dual managerial roles – corporate manager and family manager. In a study of white UK male and female managers for example, 82% of the women managers felt they faced 'greater pressures than men as managers' (Scase and Goffee, 1989). The most common major pressure reported by these women managers was associated with the conflicting demands of home and work. Scase and Goffee commented that: 'Most women managers, it seems, encounter demands which, they feel, do not affect men. "Whether married or single," comments one respondent, "a woman manager usually has the additional pressure of looking after a home. Few men realise what effect this has." (Female. Late 40s, general management).' When talking to the women managers in the sample, it became evident that like their white female counterparts, home/work conflicts were classed as major stressors (see Chapter 5). Indeed, bicultural conflict was sometimes a significant pressure for some of these women e.g. having to switch from high status in the white world of work to low status at home, such as being the third daughter-in-law in an Asian family/community (discussed more fully in Chapter 3).

The marital status and family dynamics of our sample typified that of the black and ethnic minority population within the UK (Bhavnani, 1994). The Asian women managers were likely to be married, often arranged partnerships, lived in larger households with more dependents, whereas a higher proportion of lone women parents were of Afro-Caribbean origin. However, one needs to keep in mind that where home/work conflicts did exist for the interviewees, they were not necessarily specifically culturally related and could be related to a host of factors ranging from gender role stereotyping and/or racism, to individual personality factors. These findings tend to confirm Bhavnani's (1994) assertion when she wrote:

> Easy explanations which problematise black women through reference to such factors as a fixed idea of black men's behaviour, arranged marriages, religious

restrictions and single parenting have to be questioned. The location of black women in the labour market cannot be understood by 'narrow definitions of culture' with reference to their social and family roles.

The Single Black and Ethnic Minority Woman Manager

Numerous cross-cultural studies have found that white female managers are less likely than white male managers to be married, and are less likely to have children (Larwood and Wood, 1977; Davidson and Cooper, 1992; Still, 1993). This type of profile does not match the sample of black and ethnic minority women managers, particularly those from Asian backgrounds. Only nine of the sample were living at home unattached. Of those, all but one was Afro-Caribbean and four were single parents.

The single women without children appeared to be generally happy with their unattached status and the only negative comments tended to be (like white single women managers) centred around lack of emotional and physical support: 'It sometimes would make life easier having someone to share things with. Being a single career woman the disadvantage is not having a person who you are close to, to confide in or go out with, particularly to work functions when colleagues take their partners.' However, a couple of the women managers living alone did feel isolated living in a white community, particularly if they had moved location: 'There are occasions when you'd like to talk to someone. I don't mix with people from work and I do feel I have limited social support. My friends and family live a long way away. I try and combat this by doing a lot of sport though.' Another 30 year old middle manager in education had consciously decided to live alone having tried a live-in partnership and was thriving on her choice:

> It's wonderful having your own place and living alone. I lived with someone for over a year before. I ended up doing his cooking, cleaning, looking after his kid. I was repeating the pattern that my parents had. I left and moved back to my mum's. Now I've got my own place and it's much better. You have to be strong living alone. It makes you stronger. You also develop better relationships with friends. I like my own company. It does get lonely sometimes though but – you learn to cope with that, too.

Being 'black', female and successful, was a combination which was sometimes viewed as posing difficulties in respect to finding a partner:

> I think it's very difficult to find a suitable partner as a) black men do not approach successful black women and, b) having a relationship with a white man is seen as 'selling out'. This is considered worse than doing well within a white organisation.

> Interestingly, a black friend of mine who is male, also finds that black women do not approach him because he has a high status job.

In America, Collins (1991) has hypothesised that African-American women's employment patterns may have major effects on African-American middle class families, particularly single-parent households. There are fewer African-American men than women in professional and managerial positions and hence for heterosexual women, an issue for those interested in intraracial marriage. Furthermore, African-American black women professionals are less likely to remarry than their white counterparts and according to Collins (1991): 'Another factor may be an increasing tendency by both black heterosexual women and black lesbians to head their own households and create alternative family arrangements.'

All the single parent women respondents relied heavily on their immediate and extended family, particularly parents, for support with child care. Bhavnani (1994) has suggested that compared to white women, these women may experience different access to child care, as well as racism and that these factors cut across class. While none of our interviewees with children specifically related incidences of racial discrimination in terms of child care access, like their white female managerial counterparts, feelings of guilt were occasionally voiced. This was a particular issue for one interviewee (single parent) who had made the decision for her child actually to live with her parents:

> I have felt guilty about leaving my son whilst I studied and worked. He wouldn't leave his home town or his school. However, I feel it's better for him to live in a family. It's worked out well now. He has done really well at school and is very independent. We support each other in our family, we are all very directed. We know what we want to do in life. I couldn't have got where I am now without the support and financed child care from my parents.

Having strong social and family support was also extremely important for the single working mothers when their children were ill or when they had to work away:

> It's a big conflict for me when she's ill. I have no partner to juggle that responsibility with. My line manager has cats – not children! I tend to either have the day off or get family or friends to step in. My problem as a single parent however is not so much about every day work, but having to work away sometimes. Not having a partner in those circumstances can be a real hindrance – it isn't easy.

The Black and Ethnic Minority Woman Manager – Married or Living in a Partnership

In respect to organisational attitudes the married male manager tends to be viewed as an asset, whereas the married female managers are a liability (Davidson and Cooper, 1992; Vinnicombe and Colwill, 1995). Previous research on married white women managers revealed that 47% maintained that being married had proved a disadvantage to them in terms of their career development and advancement. The disadvantages that the women themselves identified included:

- role conflict between running a home/raising children and a career;
- not being geographically mobile;
- not having enough time to run a home and career;
- feelings of guilt about not being a good wife/mother;
- lack of emotional and domestic support from their husband;
- having to take work home with them.

(Davidson and Cooper, 1992)

Many of these issues were also raised as being problematic for the sample of black and ethnic minority women managers. However, once again strong extended family support systems tended to act as an important stress buffer for many: 'I rely heavily on my family to take care of my son. His granddad picks him up from school, looks after him if he's ill and even cooks his tea. The fact that my husband's a teacher and has school holidays is also a great help.'

Tracing the history of African-American women's experiences in families, Collins (1991) points out that before enslavement, African women combined work and family without seeing a conflict between the two. African-American female farmers dominated agricultural societies and female farmers' children accompanied their mothers both in the fields and when carrying out business in the marketplace. Enslaved African women in America continued to combine child care and work, only this time they were economically exploited, their labour benefited their white owners and they lost power and control (Collins, 1991). Moreover, in the early part of the century, African-American women were in the workforce and having to balance work and family, often because their spouses were discriminated against and could not find adequate work.

However, in terms of home/work conflicts, a number of specific issues arose for the sample of female managers in partnerships, which had not been viewed as prominent in the white female management literature. These involved issues concerning mixed racial partnerships, earning more than one's partner, failure to produce male heirs, religious and cultural gender role conflicts regarding domestic help and child care.

The latest British census results reveal that more than 40% of young black and ethnic minority men who are in relationships are married to, or live with, a white partner. Marshall (1994) in her writings about social construction of black and ethnic minority female sexuality, believes that the decision to have a white partner is extremely problematic taking into account the history of their sexual oppression by white men. She quotes an interview with a female British student who said:

It's more acceptable in the black community for black men to go out with white women than for black women to go out with white men. It's all about control and power. A black man is seen as the one who controls the relationship and so his 'race' isn't being down-trodden and trampled. But if a black woman does the same thing, she is being submissive.

(Marshall, 1994)

In writing about inter-racial marriage in America, Hooks (1990) proposes that African-American women often resist marrying white men because they cannot cope with the harassment and persecution by both black and white people. Of the two Indian women managers who had married white men, both of them said they'd encountered problems, particularly from their respective families: 'Besides our families finding it difficult to cope with, our religions, culture and race sometimes clash. It's not always accepted by other people either.'

Interestingly, all but one of the the sample who were living in a partnership had white partners (one a white female). The women came from a cross section of ethnic backgrounds and two were biracial. One of the women managers from a mixed ethnic background did not view her live-in relationship with a white man as a problem as she tended to see herself more as white and felt she looked mediterranean. The other however, had been in a long term relationship with a white working class male and had encountered problems:

He was brought up in a black school and is therefore used to being in a minority situation. He is very aware and thoughtful. However, other people's perceptions can be a problem. His friends were surprised that I had a good job and his family had doubts about the relationship and sometimes I have downtrodden him, because I am so desperate not to be oppressed. We share similar experiences because he was in care when he was younger and saw a lot of violence.

One highly successful Afro-Caribbean woman manager described how her white live-in partner viewed her very much as a status symbol:

When we're together, we do get a lot of attention in public and it can cause problems. He wants to show me off – I'm 'a catch', he's proud of me and that all makes me defensive. I'm desperately worried that I might become financially dependent on him at some stage. He has this thing about black women and he's thirteen years older than me.

I still don't really understand how white men think. He doesn't understand I need to sit for hours sometimes in the total quiet. I use social support nevertheless for all my support – I have become very bicultural and mix with both.

To live and survive in a culture which is not your own is a great skill.

The lesbian interviewee who lived with a white woman partner, had formerly been married to a white man. Bhavnani (1994) emphasised the lack of research in both disabled and lesbian black and ethnic minority women in the workplace. She had chosen not to disclose openly her sexuality at work but had done so in a more discreet way 'I did not tell them I was a lesbian but most people in the department know now through my writings.'

Some research has revealed that white woman managers report problems which can arise when they overtake their husbands in terms of salary and status (Davidson and Cooper, 1992). What was interesting in our sample of black women managers, was that compared to previous findings of white female managerial populations, a high proportion, just under 60%, of those in a live-in partnership, including marriage, earned more and were in higher status jobs than their partners. This would appear to back American research findings which suggest African-American women professionals are more likely to earn more than their ethnic male counterparts (Collins, 1991). As with white women managers, for some of the sample of interviewees it was a problem either for them or their partner:

> I earn more than him. He says it isn't a problem but I think he'd like to contribute more than he does. I paid for our American holiday and I know he felt uncomfortable about that.

> It's difficult for men who see themselves as the breadwinner to cope with a high earning wife. I never saw him as the main breadwinner so it hasn't been a problem for me – just him.

> I earn more than him and it's a problem for me not for him. It makes me feel uncomfortable – he won't let me spend my money on him even though there are times when I want to. When we first met – we were the same status wise. Since then, I've doubled my money and status compared to him.

For white women managers, one of the major stressors has been linked to whether to marry/live with someone and whether to start a family (Davidson and Cooper, 1992). Decisions related to marriage/partnership were not viewed as common stressors for the women managers interviewed, although starting a family was sometimes deemed as being viewed negatively by employers. One African woman working in the private sector and living with her black boyfriend said:

> I can see that if we start a family in the next couple of years it could be a disadvantage career-wise. Once we're married, it might be assumed by people at work that I am to be perceived differently. I heard on the grapevine that they had thought of secondment for me abroad, but they might now be reconsidering, now I'm settling down!

Nevertheless, for some of the Asian women managers, a unique stressor not found in the white managerial female literature concerned the pressure to produce a male heir:

> My main home pressure is to do with the fact that we have two daughters and no son. I feel great pressure from the Asian community to have a son and some from my husband – as he won't even discuss it! He knows that I find it a

painful subject, so as I said he deliberately does not mention it. I know that he would dearly like a son – I'm resisting but I'm not sure for how long.

Like the majority of married white female managers (Davidson and Burke, 1994), the majority of women managers interviewed maintained they spent more time on home/child care duties. This parallels the findings of The British Attitudes Survey (HMSO, 1991) which found that in dual-earner couples, which constitute 60% of the total, compared to only 43% in 1973, where both partners worked full-time, women are still mainly responsible for domestic duties in 67% of households. Although British research indicates that compared to a decade ago, fathers are spending more time with their children, the majority of men remain attached to their role of the breadwinner, and job segregation based on gender still persists even in the home environment (HMSO, 1991). Interestingly, where there is an economic power shift from the breadwinner, this is when there is more likelihood of a shift towards equality in help with domestic duties. This was illustrated by two of our high earning Afro-Caribbean interviewees:

> I earn more than my husband and neither of us minds that. I believe by being married, having a family and a career, I can 'have it all'. My husband and I share everything 50–50. He does all the ironing and he's brilliant. I take the children to nursery in the morning and he picks them up and cooks for them. Every other week we swap child care versus cooking and take it in turns to take time off work if either of the children are ill. We have no real extended family where we live and that would have made life easier. We do rely on good friends and good parents though.

> Earning more, we accept that my career comes first. While I was gaining my qualifications, my husband took the dominant role in the home. I feel that he was comfortable caring for the children and dealing with the home duties. Once we moved to the UK my husband had to look after the children, whilst in the Caribbean, my mother had been able to help in this respect. He fed and bathed them, and so on. I did not feel guilty about this, we are still a very close family.

Even so, for some of the women interviewees, their cultural traditional role of women as regards home and child care duties was strong, regardless of ethnicity. This was exemplified by an Afro-Caribbean manager who described some of the cultural gender role inconsistencies in her partnership:

> I tend to concentrate and enjoy cooking. In Nigeria though, women are expected to be in charge of the household. My fiancé wouldn't dream of going into the kitchen if his friends were there. If I'm in a social gathering with Nigerians, the women serve the men. I don't like it, but I wouldn't want him to look different so I do it. We behave differently when we're alone, however.

Finally, one of the Muslim interviewees voiced concern about how her emphasis on career had had possible detrimental effects on her children and how child care had sometimes meant using non-Muslim carers:

I did feel guilty when the children were young, yes. Then two or three years ago, I felt guilt again when my son developed a social drinking problem. I couldn't understand it. I had to talk myself out of it and he did as well. When they were younger it was a juggling act. My husband rearranged his holidays, used friends to stay and so on. We would pay for the children to go away on holidays with non-faith friends – it made me sad.

CONCLUSIONS

The stories recounted by these black and ethnic minority women managers wove both similar and different childhood and current home/family experiences determined by threads leading from their ethnic origin, religion, place of birth, socio-economic background, family dynamics and parent–child and partner relationships.

These women managers currently shared many of the home/work conflicts facing their white female counterparts whether single or in a partnership. Many, particularly lone parents, relied heavily on extended family to help with child care. Additional potential pressures which seemed specific to this population included mixed racial partnerships – including racism – being more likely to earn more than one's partner, failure to produce male heirs, religious and cultural gender roles regarding domestic help and child care. Bhavnani (1994) summed the situation up aptly when she stated:

> Families may be both supportive and repressive for black women. Women of Afro-Caribbean and South Asian origin may experience differently, the operation of male dominance in the household. On the other hand, they may experience support from families whilst living in a racist society.

3

Role Conflict – Living in a Bicultural World

As a black person, you have two lives – one at work (white) and one at home (with the black community) – It's a continual split.

The previous chapter has already introduced some important issues related to the dilemmas of living in a bicultural world whether at school or in the home situation. Hence, this chapter will develop this theme by concentrating on the research literature which highlights the problems linked with the roles black and ethnic minority women managers play in their work and non-work environments. These will include the role conflicts related to the complexities involved in living in a bicultural world and the role of the token black and ethnic minority woman

In her study of 71 career-orientated African-American women, Bell (1990) revealed that these women perceived themselves as living in two specific cultural contexts, one black and the other white. In order to cope with these bicultural dimensions, the women tended to compartmentalise the different components of their lives. Bell emphasised the importance of balance in these women's bicultural images and highlighted both the strengths and weaknesses of being bicultural:

> being bicultural is a strength, providing richness and resources in a woman's life. Bicultural role conflict manifests, however, when a woman feels pressure to suppress one of her cultural identities, particularly her Afro-American identity. One woman explained:

> The white world is where I feel at the most risk. I show my white side here, which means I must be more strategic, not as spontaneous. My white side is precise and accurate. Plus, I do not want to share events from my black experience in the white world. There are no other blacks to legitimise my experiences. Most of the time I am not quick enough to put words to what I am feeling. That is what's so frustrating on the white side – not having the words to tell them how you really feel.

(Bell, 1990)

Some of the ideas in this chapter originally published by Davidson in *International Review of Women and Leadership* (1995), 1, 1.

This kind of split personality role stress was often highlighted by the women managers interviewed. One Afro-Caribbean manager in manufacturing said: 'I sometimes feel there are two of me – a side I have to show at work with the white culture which is very professional; then there's the personal side of me I reveal outside of work, which is much more ethnic.' Another female manager from the same ethnic background, described how she used support from the Afro-Caribbean community to help her combat this conflict:

> As a black person, you live two lives – one at work (white) and one at home (with the black community) – it's a continual split. I deliberately make sure that the black community acts as my safety net outside of work. In work, I also cultivate black people in the organisation, so they become allies and friends who won't let me down.

Therefore, Bell (1990) concluded that these women professionals experience role stress due to the persistent 'push and pull' between the varying cultural contexts in their lives. The expectations, values and norms of the predominantly white male dominated organisations in which they work are very dissimilar to other black and ethnic minority experiences/cultures. Bravette's (1994) participating action research with British black and ethnic minority women managers, also emphasised the conflict involved in the pressure to deny one's cultural heritage and the particular vulnerability of British-born 'black' female managers:

> Some (black women managers) recognised that they were walking a tightrope and that only if they adopted a monocultural (white) approach to their organisational existence, in other words deny significant portions of their black cultural heritage, could successful career progression within an organisation be even seriously aspired to. Black women managers born outside the UK (but invariably educated here) felt that especially vulnerable were the British-born blacks, socialised into a myth of meritocracy and educated into a system where racism comes at three different levels: individual, cultural and institutional. Despite these women's attempts at chameleon-like assimilation the white mainstream still rejects black people in positions of authority.
>
> (Bravette, 1994)

This view was also voiced by one of the women executives interviewed, who had been born in the Caribbean:

> I think if you're part of the background – you don't try as hard. Being different, you bring something with you from your previous culture – being black is special. I take nothing for granted. The young black women who were born here act like white women – they don't have the same anger either.

Bicultural role stress also appeared to be a particularly pronounced problem for a number of Indian women managers we interviewed, where the assigned status in the work environment was significantly higher than their home and community status. This could be due to ethnic issues related to caste, position in the family hierarchy, marital status, the role of women generally and whether you had 'provided' sons. One Indian woman who was the main breadwinner and a senior manager in the public sector complained:

> While my own family value my work, my in-laws don't. I don't always get my kids to bed by 7.30 p.m. as I'm not often home until 7 p.m. In their eyes (my in-laws) I'm not always being a good wife and mother. It's a real conflict for me. I have relative power in the day and return home to being regarded as a 'nothing'. I am the youngest daughter-in-law (and not slim and attractive either). I also have the stigma of having had daughters but not having produced sons. I can intellectually rationalise the situation I'm faced with but in reality, find the contrast almost impossible to cope with.

Another Indian female managerial interviewee commented:

> There are certain things you can't get away with with relatives which you could do at work. You can't be so assertive, especially with male Indian elders. You really do have to be schizoid. You learn to deal with it, you adapt and cope – you have to in order to survive. You just have to compromise.

Reid (1984) proposes that an additional role conflict facing black and ethnic minority women is when they have to decide between their dual identities as 'blacks' and women. A double-bind situation can result when a decision representing loyalty to one identity can cause rejection by the other group members. In America for example, Reid (1984) suggests that there has been criticism from some black and ethnic minority men suggesting that black and ethnic minority women have deserted their struggle for stamping out racism in favour of addressing the issue of sexism. On the other hand, white feminists have proposed that if 'black' women neglect the feminist movement, this will result in increased sexism within the 'black' community. Reid (1984) concludes that research evidence suggests that on the whole, black and ethnic minority women have put energies into the termination of both sexism and racism. However, Reid (1984) does pose the important question as to why there appears to be 'the constant need for black women to reaffirm their commitment to equal rights for all people'. Certainly, this can result in role conflict regarding service to the community versus career commitment.

SERVICE TO THE BLACK AND ETHNIC MINORITY COMMUNITY VERSUS CAREER COMMITMENT

For many of the British black and ethnic minority women managers interviewed, particularly those working in the public sectors, their profession satisfied both their personal needs and those of the ethnic minority community.

These findings tended to mirror those of Simpson (1984) in her study of African-American female lawyers. However, conflicts were commonly reported by attorneys who were not working in public service organisations:

> Said one attorney, who relinquished her previously espoused social commitment not to work with a large multinational corporation that had holdings in South Africa:

> When I was first offered this job, I almost didn't take it. They have holdings in South Africa and it went against my grain. But I decided that the experience that I would gain and hopefully be able to use would outweigh any taint that I might suffer or experience by participating in the corporation's 'evil' activities . . . Possibly if I worked there I could do a good turn . . . I think to an extent maybe it's good that a couple of us work closely with the establishment.

> Once the job pitted me against a black woman in a human rights hearing. I represented management. She was labour. I felt very odd . . . I went to court in fear and trembling about how I was to do this and how she would react to me. When she saw me, her reaction was one of amazement and joy. Those of us who went to school in the sixties got a somewhat skewed view of [how] the people . . . would feel about us as part of the establishment. The woman was very pleased that I had this particular position of responsibility.

> (Simpson, 1984)

These African-American female lawyers often spoke about feeling a sense of guilt and having 'sold out' when they left the public service for the corporate world. According to Simpson (1984): 'In their positions, they are unique individuals, minorities in a majority-ruled occupational sphere, "marginal women", removed from populations they were once dedicated to serve.'

In their study of predominantly 'black' African-American male managers, Dickens and Dickens (1991) reported this sense of having deserted the black community and 'sold out' to the whites. They found this to be particularly the case with successful 'black' managers who were very much in the minority at that seniority of management and/or those who were the first 'black' to be promoted to that particular position:

> Black managers who became successful are aware of additional burdens with which their white peers do not have to contend. Moving up in the white corporation, some blacks became concerned over how they are viewed by others of their cultural group. They fear that they may be seen as part of the establishment, having deserted the brotherhood or sisterhood.

> (Dickens and Dickens, 1991)

Interestingly, a few of the interview sample, who had chosen to take jobs related to equal opportunities or community or ethnic minority issues in the public sector, often felt tremendous conflict and isolation. They experienced role conflict related to where their allegiance lay e.g. the council versus the ethnic minority community as illustrated by the following two quotations:

> I was in great role conflict, I felt stranded in the middle between the black

community and the council. In the end, I had to draw boundaries for the sake of my own sanity.

I feel my Asian community think I'm now not really Asian, that 'she's sold out' – 'she's more on their (white council) side than the Asian side'. That makes me feel very isolated as my job and personal commitment is to help the ethnic minority community.

THE ROLE OF THE TOKEN BLACK AND ETHNIC MINORITY WOMAN

When women comprise less than 15% of a total category in an organisation, Kanter (1977) argued that they can be labelled 'tokens', as they would be viewed as symbols of their group rather than as individuals. Numerous recent studies have found that professional and managerial *white* women in token positions experience additional stresses not felt by dominant members of the same organisational status (Davidson and Cooper, 1992; White, Cox and Cooper, 1992; Still, 1993). Black and ethnic minority women managers are not only more likely to constitute an even lower percentage of managers compared to their white female counterparts, but face the double burden of being seen as symbols of both their race and their gender. The disadvantages which have been associated with being the token *white* women include:

- high visibility;
- performance pressure and being a test case;
- lack of role models and isolation (including exclusion from male groups);
- distortion of women's behaviour by others in order to fit them into pre-existing stereotypes.

The black and ethnic minority token women manager is much more likely to experience *intensified negative effects* associated with her tokenism compared to her white female counterpart. This was certainly confirmed from the analysis of the qualitative data based on the interviews with the 30 black and ethnic minority female managers. Figure 3.1 illustrates the reported major problems of being a black female manager in order of frequency of response.

Clearly, black and ethnic minority token women managers are having to cope with the double negatives associated with both racism and sexism. For the majority of interviewees, they viewed their colour as being a greater barrier/problem than their gender. In addition, many of the major problems were linked to their role of the token black woman i.e.

- performance pressure;
- racial stereotyping;
- isolation and lack of same colour role models;

1. **Performance pressure, e.g.**
   - constantly justifying professional status;
   - high expectations;
   - proving yourself more than white women;
   - credibility testing;
   - people just seeing 'black', not looking at contribution, having to sell yourself constantly
   - others (whites) being suspicious of you and expecting you to fail.

2. **Not being taken seriously/under-valued/lack of recognition (due to colour).**

3. **Racial stereotyping, e.g.**
   - others expecting you to be aggressive/subservient;
   - struggling to keep one's identity;
   - fitting into others' unconventional images/stereotypes;
   - unable to be oneself.

4. **Isolation (related to colour).**

5. **Visibility (related to colour).**

6. **Lack of support from others (whites).**

7. **Tokenism and ghettoisation (related to colour).**

8. **Lack of other black female role models.**

9. **Being a test case for future black women.**

10. **Not knowing how other whites perceive you regarding their racial attitudes.**

11. **White supervisors not understanding your special problems.**

Figure 3.1   Reported major problems of being a black and ethnic minority female manager – the double burden of racism and sexism

- visibility;
- tokenism and ghettoisation;
- being a test case for future black and ethnic minority women managers. (See Figure 3.1.)

Performance Pressure

One of the problems most frequently cited by the interview sample concerned performance pressure, having to prove oneself more than white women and the pressure of having to sell oneself constantly (see Figure 3.1). A senior executive Asian woman complained: 'As an Asian woman, I feel I have to do my job much, much better. I have to prove myself again and again. I feel I've got to be more assertive. I've got to be noticed.' Two Afro-Caribbean women, both in middle management asserted:

> People see black – they don't look at your contribution. I want to be better at my job because I'm female and black. I tend to focus on 'ethnic' rather than 'female', because there are so few of us.

> I feel I have tremendous pressure on me to perform well. I think it's because there are preconceived ideas about racial stereotypes and performance. For example, this idea white people seem to have about black people always being late. Well, I am! However, it's not because I'm black, it's due to the enormous demands of my job!

This type of performance pressure felt by ethnic minority female professionals was also illustrated by Williams (1989) in her study of African-American female college administrators. The majority of the sample, 37 (68%), felt that a black female administrator had to work twice as hard as her male counterparts. Moreover, American studies on black and ethnic minority female managers suggest that this sort of pressure is even more intensive and these women have to be bright and more talented than either their white or black male counterparts (Essed, 1991).

Essed (1991) confirms that black and ethnic minority women managers have to meet higher demands and performance levels than any other group and do not get the same promotional opportunities as white women managers:

> Compared with black and white men, they have to be better qualified, more articulate, and more aggressive, and they need more stamina to face inevitable set backs and fewer opportunities for promotion. Yet, they have to conform to the ideal of white femininity, which means that they cannot afford to appear threatening.
>
> (Essed, 1991)

Resisting Gender/Racial Stereotyping – the 'Black Mama' and 'Timid Asian Flower'

Gilkes (1990) investigated childhood, educational, occupational, and cultural experiences of 25 UK black and ethnic minority women community workers in a northern city by in-depth interviews. She concluded that all her interviewees spoke of a feeling of victimisation originating from isolation, inequality, and the status degradation fostered by negative images and stereotypes.

Stereotyping is the process of categorising an individual into a particular group, and attributing a set of characteristics to the individual on the basis of the group membership. Sex role stereotypes related to management seem to evolve from the common views of males as more independent, task-oriented, objective and generally better able than females to handle managerial responsibilities. Davidson and Cooper (1992) reported that the majority of white female managers at all levels of the hierarchy, are often pressurised into adopting certain sex stereotyped roles at work. These include the 'mother earth role', becoming 'one of the boys', the 'pet', the 'sex-object' and so on.

Schein's research has consistently reaffirmed that male managers continue to hold the same stereotypical views of the managerial job requirements i.e. 'to think manager – think male' (Schein and Davidson, 1993; Schein, 1994 – see Chapter 6). However, analysis of the interview data from our 30 black and ethnic minority female managers, consistently revealed that this stereotypical phrase should be changed to 'think manager – think *white* male'. Interestingly, the majority of the sample when questioned about both gender and racial role stereotyping alignment at work, commonly complained of role imposition based primarily on the stereotypical image of females of their *specific ethnic origin*. For example, Afro-Caribbean and African women managers, often complained of the role expectation linked to the stereotypical image of the 'aggressive, black female mama', as typified by the following comments:

> Being 'big' (and a black woman) people tend to expect me to be aggressive. I often shock them as I tend to be gentle. I do, however, use a deep voice to suit on occasions. I won't adjust to how men 'want' me to behave.

> I am in an area where I am not expected to be because it is white and male dominated. I have to understand the men that I am dealing with and the organisation as a whole. This power threatens people. People trust me though and this helps me, although I do suppress my sexuality. Most of my team know I am lesbian. I tend to be fairly asexual. I won't play earth mother i.e. the mammy role.

Another Afro-Caribbean interviewee described how she had taken positive steps to ensure that her behaviour was assertive rather than aggressive: 'I now *know* I am assertive. However, because of my race I am still accused of being aggressive. I have used T.A., worked on my voice and my body language. I chose to be firm and feel more confident about my behaviour.' Conversely, many of the Asian women we interviewed felt they were expected to conform to the stereotypical 'female timid Asian flower' role alignment:

> Being Asian, I'm expected to be submissive but in reality, I'm totally opposite. I do have an arranged marriage but many whites find this hard to cope with and say to me – 'but you don't seem the type to do that' – What 'type' am I supposed to be? I'm not here to educate people's strange expectations.

> With groups such as the police force – it tends to be assumed that I am an 'unassertive, dumb, Asian bimbo'. To counteract this I wear a particular suit, glasses and only a touch of make-up. I will not use sexual manipulation and I am clear and direct. Whilst it does not undermine my self-worth – I do feel that I need to work twice as hard to be taken seriously.

In addition, being treated paternalistically and in a patronising manner was another common complaint as illustrated by an Indian personnel manager in her early thirties, who had developed her own defence mechanism to cope:

> Half of the white managers I deal with are paternalistic towards me. If I

became the real 'me', then they became even more paternalistic. I tend, therefore, to hide behind a tough persona. They end up knowing nothing about me,
my personal life, whether I'm angry or fed up, nothing. As a defence mechanism I hide any feelings – it saves me from getting hurt.

Certainly, it is not easy resisting role assignment but what is evident is that
compared to her white female counterpart, the black and ethnic minority
woman is having to cope with the pressures of *both* gender and ethnic
stereotyping role imposition – once again, a double burden.

Isolational and Lack of Black and Ethnic Minority Female Role Models

Compared with white women, black and ethnic minority women managers
in token positions are even less likely to have role models they can emulate
and turn to for support and guidance (Bell, 1990; Essed, 1991). As a consequence, they are more likely to complain of feeling isolated and missing
support from black peers. Essed (1991) viewed lack of black and ethnic
minority role models and isolation from other ethnic women as major structural problems encountered by these women both in higher education and in
securing and keeping jobs. In her study of black and ethnic minority women
community workers in the UK, Gilkes (1990) found that many of these
women discussed their feelings of isolation which tended to encourage them
to develop an interdependent approach to their problems. Indeed, one of the
female managers interviewed had left her last job due to the racism and
isolation she experienced: 'The isolation drove me mad. I found it impossible to cope with the racism without support. I felt so alone.' This isolation
has also been linked to being omitted from important support networks
which could help enhance one's professional skills (Williams, 1989; Bell,
1990). For example, 42% of Williams' (1989) African-American female
American college administrators felt somewhat excluded from the information and support network. Williams (1989) emphasised the relevance of this
finding by stating:

> The support network and the feeling of being part of the administrative team
> is important for an individual's success since the feeling of team involvement
> centres around the concept of trust. If there is a feeling that decisions will be
> made from established criteria and that the rules will not be changed in
> midstream, an administrator can concentrate on the task at hand rather than
> trying to figure out what the new rules are.
>
> (Williams, 1989)

This was reaffirmed by one of our interviewees, an Asian women who
commented 'If there had been other black people, it would have been so
much easier. There is no precedent to follow.'

A number of our female ethnic minority managers also highlighted
feelings of isolation at work due to cultural differences related to dress,

communication, interests and verbal and non-verbal behaviour. An Afro-Caribbean female administrative officer described her experiences:

> I have to suppress the way I really am. I have different interests and sense of humour and therefore often keep quiet. I have totally different perspectives on such issues as alcohol and sex for example – sometimes I find myself having to adapt in order to not feel totally isolated. For this reason, I don't always socialise with my white colleagues. This annoys me though, as I do feel cut off. The others in this office are different from me. I feel it – they feel it.

Certainly, for Asian women managers in particular, their religion, which prohibits alcohol, was often viewed as a factor facilitating isolation from white colleagues. One senior executive Muslim Asian woman viewed her gender, race and religion, as being factors which not only isolated her, but prevented her from reaching director level:

> Being Muslim sets me apart. I can't go out for drinks, which is a big disadvantage and there are also times when I fast, which means no business lunches. I sometimes go to the pub with my work colleagues but after they've had a few drinks, I feel left out and often leave. I've been told I'll never be considered at director level as all the directors are male and would feel uncomfortable with me there – they do most of their dealings over meals and alcoholic drinks. If I joined them – it would rock the boat.

American research literature indicates that black and ethnic minority female professionals and managers tend to quote important role models as often being someone not associated with their work environments (Williams, 1989). For example, Epstein's (1973) early study of African-American women professionals, found many gave mother–provider figures such as mothers and grandmothers, as important role models. These women generated strong, independent, positive images as women as 'doers' regardless of the type of employment they had. Williams' (1989) sample of African-American female college administrators all identified a black role model from their youth with whom they had formed a strong identification. These included teachers, a parent, a relative and in some cases black sororities such as Alpha Kappa Alpha and Delta Sigma Theta.

Lack of black and ethnic minority female role models was certainly a problem emphasised by our managerial sample (see Figure 3.1). However, like their American counterparts, many of the women quoted important role models from outside their work environment. In fact, mother–provider figures as role models were particularly common for the Afro-Caribbean women managers. These women often described the strong prominent role Caribbean women tend to play in the family environment e.g. 'The women in my family have all been extremely powerful role models – they live their lives to the full and were all successful.' Nevertheless, while many of the interviewees actively acted as role models for other black and ethnic minority women, one or two emphasised the extra energy and effort this entailed:

People like me not only act as role models for other black women managers but also the black community see that women can actually achieve something, other than running a home. Unfortunately, there are not enough of us. We tend to spend time and energy finding each other. I gladly act as a role model for many black women. However, they do tend to sap me – I'm continually being telephoned by black women as I'm in such a prominent position.

Visibility

Token women are also subject to three 'peripheral tendencies'; those associated with, unsuitability, contrast and assimilation (Kanter, 1977). Indeed, being female in management and being from an ethnic minority exposes these female executives to extremes of high visibility (Iles and Auluck, 1991). They are always bathed in a glaring spotlight. In the words of Epstein (1973):

These ascribed sex (female) and race (black) statuses are dominant; they are visible and immutable and impose severe limits on individuals' capacities to alter the dimensions of their worlds and the attitudes of others towards them. In the elite professions, blacks and women have been considered inappropriate and undervalued, and as a result they have constituted only a tiny proportion of the prestigious professionals. Not only have they been prevented from working in the elite professions, but the few who do manage to become professionals tend to work in the less remunerative and prestigious subfields.

Almost all the women managers interviewed viewed themselves as highly visible in their organisation, much more so than their white female counterparts. For some, this brought disadvantages such as loss of privacy, mistakes being highlighted and getting attention for their 'discrepant' sex and ethnic characteristics, rather than for their skills. This often meant having to put extra effort into getting taken seriously, e.g.

I am highly visible in the company and I have to work through that. You tend to be on your best behaviour and need to be always prepared. I'm set up as 'the example'. I feel pressure from both management and the community, they try and manipulate me – they even try and dictate what I wear, how I wear my hair – even try and put appointments in my diary without my permission – hang on a minute, what's going on?

A number of women also complained that while they often wanted to discuss racial issues (including in reference to themselves) white colleagues and superiors usually evaded the issue and preferred: 'not to discuss such things as they obviously felt highly uncomfortable – a taboo topic.'

Nevertheless, high visibility need not always be a negative factor. All of the 31 African-American female lawyers interviewed by Epstein (1973) felt that their colour and being female enhanced their career aspirations and gave them opportunities they may well not have had, had they been 'only women' or 'only black'. Being 'black' and female gave these attorneys a unique status combination making them extremely visible and ensuring that news of 'good performances' spread speedily throughout the law fraternity. Interestingly, many of the more successful female executives interviewed had deliberately used their 'unique status combination' as an important career advancement strategy: 'Visibility definitely works to my advantage – also my name is different and if I do some work and present it, it stirs up interest – I strive to project a professional image. I have even been picked to feature in company videos shown to the directors.'

Tokenism and Black and Ethnic Minority Jobs

Iles and Auluck (1991) maintained that black and ethnic minority professionals in Britain are often steered away from the main career tracks and sidelined into routine 'token' 'showcase' or 'black' jobs in areas such as personnel, welfare, dealing with black staff, customers or clients or in equal opportunity units. Certainly, many of our interviewees complained of pressures associated with this type of racial tokenism. One director in the Health Service isolated her major problem as: 'being a black woman and consequently being discounted. It's a stress always having to prove that you are not a fluke, that you are only in the position you are because they needed a token black woman.'

Another Asian female project manager felt her tokenism was being exploited to the extent that she was supposed to be a 'race expert', even though her specific job had nothing to do with racial issues: 'I definitely feel I have been assigned the role of the token *black* woman manager. I especially feel this working in a white organisation, as opposed to an all *black* team before. Everything to do with race is dumped on you – you're expected to have all the answers!'

Being a Test Case For Future Black and Ethnic Minority Women Managers

Numerous research studies on white women managers have isolated a particular burden associated with being token women: the pressures related to being a test case for the employment of future women in the company at management level (Harnett and Novarra, 1979; Davidson and Cooper, 1992). Bell (1990) also points out that compared to white women managers, these women are much more likely to be the first of their race and gender to have held a middle or upper level management position in the organisation. Indeed, 63% of our sample were the first of their race and gender in their particular job.

Not surprisingly, the pressures associated with being a test case for future black and ethnic minority women managers are often a tremendous burden, as illustrated by the following quotations from some of our interviewees:

I am a test case if black women are going to proceed into senior management. I'm definitely being watched. Unfortunately, no-one has told me the rules but I have to keep on playing anyway!

(Caribbean female senior manager, private sector.)

My major problem is being a test case and having to constantly justify my professional status. In addition, I have to continue doing this within the full glare of the organisation. You are breaking new ground and have no point of references.

(Indian female personnel officer, public sector.)

I feel under enormous pressure to perform well. White people always seem to be looking to me to fail. If I fail though, I let down all black women. I feel this is a big responsibility.

(Caribbean female middle manager, health services.)

For one Afro-Caribbean female middle manager in her early thirties, this 'test-case' pressure had become too much to cope with and she had decided to quit her job and start her own business.

I felt enormous performance pressure from both my friends and colleagues as well as from myself. I thought people expected a lot from me being the first black woman manager. I tried too hard to perform well and have worn myself out. I'm leaving . . . moving on. I never want to work for anyone else ever again.

CONCLUSIONS

Clearly, the material presented in this chapter illustrates that compared to their white female counterparts, black and ethnic minority British women managers live in a bicultural world and face even greater role conflict. They:

- face the double negative effects of sexism and racism and are more likely to be in token and test-case positions;
- have fewer if any role models, and are more likely to feel isolated and visible;
- contend with stereotypical images based on gender and ethnic origin;
- are more likely to experience performance pressure;
- have greater home/social/work conflicts, particularly in terms of their role conflict with regards to the family and the black community.

It should also be noted that once again, women managers from different ethnic minority backgrounds and religions share both similar and dissimilar experiences. Asian and Afro-Caribbean female managers for example, have very different cultural/community/family traditions and also have to face different ethnic stereotyping role impositions, both inside and outside the work environment. These findings reaffirm Bhavnani's (1994) assertion when she states: 'Nor should the experience of black women be assured to

be the same in all contexts. For there is an immense diversity and differen-
tiation within the overall category of black women generated by such
factors as ethnicity and national origin.'

Finally, Bravette (1994) aptly summarised the issue of bicultural
competence and black and ethnic minority women managers when she
wrote:

> Truly biculturally competent individuals will have an understanding of what is
> being taken as, or conversely, what is being given up as they seek to achieve.
> Black managers in organisations need to address this issue of biculturality: is it
> possible to be truly bicultural without being grounded in the culture with
> which an individual has common racial heritage? Evidence shows the answer
> to be no! Only with the above grounding can an individual even hope to
> become bicultural with their integrity intact having made informed choices.

4

Relationships at Work – Racial Taboos and Negative Stereotypes

I recently attended a meeting with a few of my male colleagues (all white). At one point, one of them suddenly exclaimed, 'I think we have a problem here, definitely a nigger in the wood pile!' I couldn't believe what I was hearing. What made it worse, was that nobody else seemed to even notice what he'd said. He certainly didn't . . .

Studies indicate that being in a minority, white female managers face particular difficulties and problems in their relationships at work (Davidson and Cooper, 1992; Vinnicombe and Colwill, 1995). However, for black and ethnic minority women women managers, support relationships in organisations are usually more scarce (Denton, 1990) and these women have to cope with the dynamics of both sexism and racism in interpersonal relationships and interactions. This chapter will examine the complexities linked with relationships at work for black and ethnic minority women managers and include relationships and social support issues concerning superiors, colleagues and subordinates, as well as sexual harassment. Finally, one needs to broach the subject of communication, an essential ingredient of any form of relationship.

RELATIONSHIPS WITH SUPERIORS

In an American study aimed at discovering the primary obstacles encountered by African-American female managers in the interaction with the corporate culture, White (1990) concluded that the majority of senior management officials, predominately white males, regarded senior jobs as being too difficult and technical for 'black' women. According to White (1990): 'Black women are often perceived by senior management as being incapable of supervising large numbers of people, a large proportion being men who may resent black women who are above them in the corporate hierarchy.'

One Indian woman manager interviewed in the sample, working with predominantly white employees, found her only way of coping with relationships at work was to be tough and never reveal her true self:

I hide behind a tough persona. Others at work don't know anything about me or my life – I don't show my feelings. I never show that I feel fed up, or don't agree with their comments and so on. Its my defence mechanism – I save myself from getting hurt this way.

Another believed that she was only accepted by whites by becoming (in their eyes) an honorary white:

People tend to assume when they first meet me that I'm not the one in authority. They usually have to 'white wash' me before they can deal with me. Because I'm middle class and have been properly educated, they often treat me as white – with mitigating circumstances! I become to them – an honorary white.

I have to admit, I am suspicious of white people who I think are often two-faced. I always assume that people are racist, I'm afraid, until they prove otherwise.

Collins (1991) proposes that while white women have been offered a share of the white male power on the condition that they agree to remain subordinate, for women, the historical relationship with white men has been one of rejection. Hence, Collins found that white men have tended to reject, exploit and objectify African-American women.

The most common complaint about relationships between the black and ethnic minority women managers in the sample and their superiors, revolved around racial and sexual discriminations. A young female middle manager highlighted her dilemma:

My main problems at work stem from my poor relationship with my white, middle class male boss. He continuously bombards me with racist and sexist comments. He's totally unsympathetic to maternity leave, family commitments etc. I do confront any inappropriate comments by saying 'I don't like that'. I do try to be assertive rather than aggressive. However, being young can also prove a problem – it isn't easy.

Alternatively, another interviewee facing similar relationship problems with her white boss felt it safer not to challenge such remarks: 'One of my white male bosses always chaired important meetings and, like his predecessor, would always put me down by calling me "pet". I wanted to challenge him but realised this man could affect my career, so I never did even though it really bothered me.'

Greenhaus *et al.*'s (1990) research into supervisors' attributed job performance ratings reported that when ethnic minorities or women performed well, it tended to be attributed to help from others or luck, rather than ability. On the other hand, when white males did well, supervisors were more likely to attribute this to ability. They concluded that 'black women managers are penalised twice, because not only are performance appraisals affected, the superior–subordinate interaction is also affected' (Greenhaus *et al.*, 1990).

This type of double penalisation from white male superiors was voiced by an Indian woman interviewee working in the public sector

> My new line manager has really affected my confidence. He recently suggested I wasn't doing my job well. He is a sexist and also he has never managed a black person before – I felt he thought I was just a token position. I had to learn how to operate him – work out his dynamics. When I eventually confronted him as I couldn't cope with his behaviour anymore, he said he was frightened of me.

Some women spoke of withdrawal of support from white superiors, which was particularly harrowing for a black woman in Personnel who had to sack a white male due to his racism:

> There was a white guy who had been here for five years. He was racist and everybody complained about him – but nothing had been done. I tried to help him and gave him warnings, but in the end I had no choice but to sack him. I didn't like doing it, but it had to be done. He then took us to an Industrial Tribunal. The Directors withheld their support for me at this point. They questioned me and appeared to doubt my action and decision. I needed their support but they left me out on a limb. I could have lost my job. Only after I defended my action and won did they congratulate me. It was too late then. I felt if I had been white, I would have got their support. I believe they wanted me to fail.
>
> Even the other staff who had initially complained about the guy, were not supportive. I think they thought the same thing could happen to them and started to say everything I did was wrong. At this point, I even started to doubt myself. I felt totally alone and alienated and this is when my depressions etc. started.

Superiors Feeling Threatened

Interestingly, compared to white female managers, the women interviewed were much more likely to comment that they believed their superiors viewed them as a threat regardless of their bosses' gender or ethnic background and a typical reaction was

> I am a threat to the director, a white female, who is terrified of me. She has her directorship out of patronage. I and she knows, I should really have her job. I have never even been in her office – she is so territorial. She is a friend of the chairman. However, she needs me. I had a really difficult time with her initially as she deliberately overworked me.

Another interviewee complained:

> I get the impression white females have to prove something if you challenge them. They don't like it. White women have cliquey groups to protect them- selves rather than 'networks'. I think they are threatened by me – if I challenge

my white female boss, she gets very upset. In all honesty, I don't see why she should.

A number of our interview sample quoted instances of ethnic minority male bosses feeling uncomfortable and threatened by them. One Afro-Caribbean woman had been forced to leave her job because of the negative effects of such a relationship:

> My worst experience with a superior was undoubtedly the terrible time I had with a black male boss. He just couldn't cope with black successful women. In the end, I had to quit and decided to start up my own business. Ironically, he could just about deal with high flying white women but women from his own ethnic background were a 'no, no' as far as he was concerned.

When there is interaction between a 'black' person and a white person, Dickens and Dickens (1991) described the dynamics of such interactions as being pivoted on the three dimensions – power, control and trust. Power is centred around and is held by the white person, who is a member of the dominant culture. There is little trust because there is probably little common base of personal experience as well as no common base of cultural experience. In addition, the fear or threat felt by the white person is often centred around their fear of losing control.

The word 'taboo' is often littered in the literature when cross-sex and cross-race relationships in the work environment are discussed. Thomas (1989) for example, quotes the description given by a white male engineer when he had a new 'black' female subordinate join his working group

> I was told that Kathy shared my special interests in product design, but I also found that I was staying away from her. I hooked up with all the other new junior people, but not with her. Finally, I approached her to join me on a project. I knew I was attracted to her. When I spoke she responded warmly, but I was also aware of a hesitancy in me, that I wanted to withdraw. It was as if a taboo was operating.

Thomas (1989) concluded that individuals find it difficult to discuss a taboo as taboos both forbid action as well as forbidding *reflecting* on what is forbidden. Consequently,

> the racial taboo described above – the creation of a liaison between a white man and a black woman – links wider cultural processes to organisational reality while operating to suppress this linkage. It thus becomes the source of an experimental underground – a set of experiences often unconsciously enacted and rarely acknowledged which nonetheless shapes the relationships between blacks and whites in significant ways.
>
> (Thomas, 1989)

Clearly, these types of racial taboos certainly have serious consequences when examining mentoring/sponsoring relationships for black and ethnic minority women managers.

RELATIONSHIPS WITH COLLEAGUES
AND SUBORDINATES

On the whole, men who are most likely to hold prejudicial views about women as managers are either those members of the 'old school', who hold traditionalist views about women generally, or younger men who feel highly threatened by the 'infiltration' of very competent, professional women (Davidson and Cooper, 1992; Davidson, 1996). When racial as well as gender dynamics are also a factor in work relationships, then the whole process becomes more complex and potentially more difficult. As discussed in the previous chapters, many *black* female managers spoke of:

- feelings of isolation linked to bicultural role conflicts;
- problems of adaptation;
- lack of acceptance by colleagues and superiors;
- discrimination and prejudice, particularly racial.

Typical comments included:

> I feel different from others (whites) at work and this ultimately affects my rela-tionships. I tend to cope by keeping myself to myself.

> I get on with people at work, but my friends outside are completely different. It's like having a double life. My relationships at work are very work related and I do not socialise with work colleagues much. I keep my outside life very private.

An interesting finding from the interview analysis, was that many women managers complained of relationship problems with their black and ethnic minority colleagues, particularly black and ethnic minority men, which became more pronounced once they became their superior. One of the inter-viewees recalled:

> I am in charge of the office when the chief executive is away. However, my two Asian male colleagues resent this fact. I am a threat to them because I've been made in charge and they haven't, and also because I'm an Asian woman. I also have problems working with a male Sikh colleague on a joint project. He has been very difficult. He also sees me as a threat. He wants to control every-thing. He also believes that an Asian woman's place is in the home. He can't cope with a woman who is equal or superior to himself. I have explained about him to the Chief Executive. However, the man in question gets on well with the male directors and is well respected in the community. As a result – no one is prepared to do anything.

According to Thomas (1989) 'White men appropriate black women, black women can rise up by going along with this, and black men are angry and suspicious.' This type of alienation and hostility from other 'black' men was voiced by the following Afro-Caribbean female manager in Education:

> I feel stress from my own kind. If I see someone in business from my own

people, usually male, I try to make some kind of contact. I will smile at them, for example. However, they don't usually reciprocate. The whites, on the other hand, appear more friendly and forthcoming.

Occasionally, problems could also arise from some ethnic minority female subordinates who appeared to expect special concessions from a same sex, same culture boss:

> A Nigerian employee of mine made it very difficult for me in the company. She said that I was very authoritarian. Her work deteriorated and she eventually gave in her notice, fortunately, as I was going to have to sack her. She assumed that I would be an ally, but in business, I am very strict. She just wasn't able to meet the deadlines when she was supposed to.

What was evident from our interviewees was that once these women held the boss position, the main issue for their subordinates, and some colleagues, was predominantly their race with the secondary added dimension being their gender. Typical of this issue was this comment:

> My staff's main problems have been having to come to terms with the fact that I'm black – not that I'm female – and the fact that I'm a lot younger than many of them.
>
> I've coped by being consistent in how I behave, and by being myself and being true to me.

One of the most senior women executives interviewed had adopted the following rather forthright management strategy, when it came to supervising men!

> When I was younger, I did have problems supervising older (white) men. What helped me, was when I went on a management training course where I raised the problem. The woman trainer told me something I've always remembered and practised:
>
> When they come into your office, grab their balls. However, don't let them leave before returning them sugar-coated!

SEXUAL HARASSMENT

Sexual harassment can be defined as unwanted conduct of a sexual nature, or other conduct based on sex affecting the dignity of women and men at work (Rubenstein, 1991). It is a potential problem for the majority of working women and recent surveys have shown that sexual harassment is widespread. Vinnicombe and Colwill (1995) refer to an International Labour Organisation Survey of 23 countries which found 6 to 8% of employed women change jobs due to sexual harassment and 74% of British women have reported being sexually harassed at work. While the highest percentage of sexual harassment victims are female, it has been estimated that about 15% of men have suffered sexual harassment at work.

Victims of sexual harassment often experience negative behavioural, psychological, physical and health-related outcomes (Terpstra and Baker, 1991; Wright and Bean, 1993). For example, Earnshaw and Davidson's (1994) study of British women, including some managers, who had taken sexual harassment claims to Industrial Tribunals indicated that over half those interviewed had to seek medical help and were prescribed drugs such as sleeping tablets or anti-depressants. Not surprisingly the victims' relationships with others, particularly other men, can be adversely affected. So can their general attitude towards work in terms of:

• lowered motivation;
• decreased job satisfaction;
• lowered confidence to do the job;
• lowered organisational commitment

(Gutek, 1985)

Victims of sexual harassment are much more likely than the male harasser to be relocated within the company, quit or lose their job. The most frequent harasser is a woman's peer or co-worker, followed by a superior, the latter being often perceived as initiating the more severe forms of sexual harassment (Cleveland,1994).

Sexual Harassment and Women in Management

Although research shows that all women are at risk regardless of their appearance or age, certain groups of women appear to be more vulnerable to sexual harassment. According to Lach and Gwartney-Gibbs (1993) these include women who are younger, single or divorced, have a higher education and who tend to have less traditional jobs. Cleveland (1994) concludes that women in non-traditional female jobs, including managerial jobs, are more likely to experience sexual harassment. This type of sexually demeaning work environment includes threatening and hostile sexual comments, accompanied by non-sexual acts specifically intended to remind the woman she is an outsider. Lach and Gwartney-Gibbs (1993) interpret these findings as indicative of sexual harassment being a kind of retaliation against women for threatening male social and economic power.

Women in management positions are in no way immune from sexual harassment and some research suggests that they are most likely to encounter sexual harassment inflicted by co-workers, clients and subordinates, particularly when on business trips, entertaining clients or at social functions (Clarke, 1986; Cleveland, 1994). In an in-depth study of 60 British female managers, all white, the author found that 52% of the sample reported that they had experienced sexual harassment at work. In addition, women occupying middle and junior level management positions in particular, were more likely to have been victims compared to senior female executives (Davidson and Cooper, 1983). In comparison, 26.7% (8) of the black and ethnic minority female managers said they had been sexually harassed in the workplace, half of them by black and ethnic minority males and the other half by white males. Although dealing with a small sample of 30, the lower percentage of reported experiences of sexual harassment may be indicative of a combination of racial taboos and/or the 'invisibility' of ethnic minority women. For example, in Marshall's (1994) study of the social construction of British black and ethnic minority female sexuality, she stated that a small minority of her interviewees believed that their sexuality was rendered invisible. She quotes one ethnic minority woman who suggested that the invisibility of ethnic minority women in the media and British society as being the main problem, rather than derogatory sexual images *per se*. Marshall (1994) also proposed that this sexual invisibility is enhanced by the imagery which defines these women, particularly Afro-Caribbeans, as 'sexual mammies', playing the mother role (see Chapter 3). Thomas (1989) on the other hand, highlights the racial taboos linked to the creation of a liaison between a white man and a 'black' woman and the subsequent *avoidance* by black and ethnic minority women managers of vulnerable situations whereby such liaisons might occur. One of Thomas's (1989) African-American women managers exemplified this strategy by saying:

> Being seen with white men presents problems. . . . White men are kind of funny around black women and if one knows about history. . . . Actually, I should own (the problem) myself. My being seen with white men, I have a problem with it. You know, being a white man's slut and all the connotations that go with it. So when I'm away on training, I isolate myself after hours. So I have to own a piece of not feeling extremely comfortable.
>
> (Thomas, 1989)

Hooks (1990) made a similar observation about the black and ethnic minority women she taught at the University of Southern California:

> black female students discussed their fear of white men and their anger and rage that white men approached them at jobs, in restaurants, hallways, or on elevators and made sexual overtures. Most women in the class agreed that to avoid these negative encounters they are never friendly with white men, ignore them, or send hostile vibrations in their direction.

Both Collins (1991) and Hooks (1990) view the roots of these taboos as stemming from the enslavement of African-American women and the justification from both American white women and men of their sexual exploitation. Hooks (1990) believes the white Americans argued that African-American women were the initiators of sexual relationships with men. Hence, the emergence of the stereotype of 'black women as sexual savages'. Post-slavery, African-American women's domination of low paid domestic/service jobs exposed them to the constant threat of sexual harassment. Consequently, these historical origins of sexual harassment of

African-American women by white men, contributed to images and fantasies of black women as fair game for all men (Collins, 1991). These types of images are not restricted to the black African-American women. In her British study of black and ethnic minority female sexuality, Marshall (1994) said that the majority of the ethnic minority women she interviewed believed they were perceived by many men and white people as being lascivious and licentious. She postulates that these images reinforce the oppression of black and ethnic minority women and protect people who violate them from punishment. She quotes Melisa, a 26 year old office supervisor who viewed the 'black' woman as a source of eroticism in British society:

> Black women are something new and different like an exotic fruit you want to bite. You don't want to try an apple because everyone's had one. Try a kiwifruit and once one person's tried it and spread the news, then others will have a bite, scared at first but will try it.

These types of erotic fantasy stereotypes were adhered to by an Indian woman middle manager interviewed, when describing her experiences of sexual harassment:

> I was sexually harassed by a white male colleague before I got married. It was all to do with this man's fantasy he had about Asian women. He never actually touched me, but it was what he said. He saw himself as a 'lady's man'. I dealt with it by hammering him in work discussions.

An Afro-Caribbean woman manager now working in the private sector related an unpleasant incident which happened to her when she was younger:

> When I first left school, I was a printer in the Civil Service. I was only 16 and I was friendly and talked to everyone. This man (white) came in one day and walked right up to me by the machine and tried to rub my chest. I was gobsmacked – I couldn't even scream. Luckily, a woman walked into the office and he left. I told her and she told her boss who got his boss to talk to the man. Nothing happened though!

At least three women interviewees said that they fended off any forms of sexual harassment by being assertive. One Jamaican woman manager exclaimed: 'Yes – men try it on with me but they soon back off. I think my size has a lot to do with it.' Another Pakistani senior executive maintained she used a combination of assertiveness and her religion to stop verbal sexual harassment:

> I had a junior, older male (white) who consistently used bad language. He'd say things like 'computers going down like ladies' knickers'. I was assertive, told him he had to stop, and it worked. Also, perhaps because I'm a Muslim, I think I'm able to create a sort of barrier between me and others like him.

For those women we interviewed who had been sexually harassed by an ethnic minority male in the workplace, they recounted additional problems relating to intraracial taboos. A young Indian women described how she only took action because she had support from other Asian women, who were also 'victims':

> I was sexually harassed in my last job by a black man. It was very difficult to handle as it was an Asian man, a manager, and this sort of behaviour did not fit that stereotype. He was harassing a few of us and we found it a difficult situation as we didn't want to get him the sack. If I'd been on my own, I wouldn't have done anything about it.

Feagin (1992) responded to articles by Bell and colleagues in which they wrote about a famous case in America in which an African-American woman brought a case of sexual harassment by an African-American man, before the US Senate Judiciary Committee – The Anita Hill–Clarence Thomas hearings. According to Feagin:

> Bell points out that Anita Hill was in a no-win situation. By indicting a black man for sexual harassment, she was raising, in addition to the general issue of sexism, an intraracial issue whose explosive nature many white Americans would not understand. Hill was breaking the taboo on black women speaking out against what some black men do to them. As Bell underscores, Hill broke the code of silence. Bell herself violates this code by talking explicitly about the Black Men's Club, including some of the 'liberal' black male leaders who worked for the Thomas nomination behind the scenes. Ignoring the sexism of black males and emphasising the black liberation struggle as for 'black manhood', Bell argues, is wrongheaded, for it is as much a struggle for black womanhood as for black manhood.

An example of the strength of the 'Black Men's Club' was clearly illustrated by one of the female Asian managers interviewed, when she was sexually harassed by an Asian colleague:

> I was sexually harassed in my last job by an Asian colleague who also harassed other Asian women I worked with. We women banded together to start procedures against him. However, in the end we settled at requesting he be moved away as we women were put under tremendous pressure from the black community and black workers in other local authorities not to take further action. It was amazing to me just how strong the black workers' network is, even between London and Birmingham. The black community – in particular, the men – banded together against us women and in the end, we had no choice, but to comply with their wishes.

In the late 1980s, the European Commission began to show concern about workplace sexual harassment and the lack of management action to stamp it out. They commissioned a research report to determine the extent to which sexual harassment was a problem across the European Community (Rubenstein, 1988). Following the submission of this report, an EC Recommendation and Code of Practice were published, emphasising the role of both management and unions in combating and communicating procedures for dealing with sexual harassment in work settings

(Rubenstein, 1991). Effective steps which management can take to deal with the problem include:

- education and training programmes;
- clear procedures for dealing with cases of sexual harassment;
- a workplace policy which identifies sexual harassment as an unacceptable and discriminatory practice.

COMMUNICATION

Kanter (1977) has estimated that managers spend between 50% and 93% of their time in social intercourse with a third to half of their time in meetings and up to 20% of their time on the telephone. Case (1993) asserts that linguistic activity is the key to understanding managerial behaviour: 'Since the language people use and the associations they make reveal how they see and interact with their world, the experiences of women, and their increasing presence in the workforce, mandate understanding their cultural perspective and respecting their differences where they exist.'

Researchers, who have studied the language patterns and topics of women, have almost exclusively used white subjects, and have tended to differentiate between feminine and masculine speech. Generally, while masculine speech is deemed more powerful and direct, feminine speech seems indirect, accommodating and powerless (Doyle and Paludi, 1995). Lakoff (1975) suggested that feminine speech patterns, whether used by men or women, may convey a feeling of powerlessness in that they are more likely to include qualifiers, fillers, tag questions and longer request phrases. Moreover, in mixed-sex interactions, men:

- talk longer than women;
- interrupt women more than women interrupt men;
- are more likely to initiate more topics than women and have more success with their topics being developed.

(Tannen, 1990; Case, 1993, 1994)

While there is some controversy in the literature concerning some of these differences, e.g. Case (1993) quotes several studies which challenge the overuse of tag questions ('we should go, don't you think?') by women compared to men, there is a strong move to view gender differences as being just that – different rather than powerful versus powerless. Doyle and Paludi (1995) suggest that feminine speech should be viewed as valuable in fostering a more co-operative atmosphere with tag questions, for example, inviting the listener to contribute to the conversation. They also propose that several non-verbal communication strategies such as increased eye contact are more often used by women and again, encourage individuals to participate in conversation. Case (1993) concludes: 'Individual language styles themselves each have unique and positive attributes which can contribute to organisational effectiveness.'

However, with a few notable exceptions (e.g. Roberts *at al.*, 1992), there is very little published research on ethnic differences in terms of communication, particularly the implications for work environments and management. James *et al.* (1994) refer to a few studies which have proposed that attention-getting verbal and non-verbal behaviour by minority individuals can accentuate the effects of stereotypes and other precursors to discrimination and prejudice (e.g. Sullins, 1989). Fernandez (1981) for example, reported that ethnic minority workers who spoke out about perceived problems with the majority were more likely to receive more scrutiny from their co-workers. A number of the women managers interviewed mentioned both verbal and non-verbal communication differences and barriers which were inherently cultural in origin as well as being linked to ethnic stereotyping. Typical comments were:

> Communication can be a problem sometimes and I find even body language can be misinterpreted. Even though I speak perfect English, the sense of humour that white people have is still alien to me.

> I find my white colleagues tend to comply more in meetings, whereas I say what I think. I feel it is a characteristic of my culture. Also, we don't tend to chit chat. If I have nothing to say, I don't say anything. However, the others (whites) assume that I must be in a bad mood – it's a problem.

> Manners in this country are different. People coming from Asian backgrounds interact more, whereas I find people here don't ask opinions unless asked. In Pakistan, if you didn't ask, you'd be classed as being uncaring. People here tell me a problem but I feel they probably don't want my opinion. The opposite would be the case from an Asian. I still find these differences hard to cope with, even though I've been here 35 years!

> At work, I tend to use 'work speak' so I tend to get over differences and problems. Afro-Caribbeans tend to be more open about successes and failures. White colleagues seem to be reluctant to talk about their successes – they seem to emphasise the constraints and problems.

An Indian woman manager in the public sector who had a very refined English accent revealed how others (whites) were often surprised and 'taken back' at how she spoke:

> Some people assume that because you are black that you speak different languages, eat different foods, etc. I am a curiosity. When I speak to people on the phone who haven't met me, they can't quite work it all out. They ask me about my name, which is very Indian and then about my so called 'posh accent'.

Another Indian woman described her frustration over misinterpretation of both verbal and non-verbal communication: 'When I say "yes", I sometimes mean "yes – I heard you", not necessarily "yes – I agree with you". My non-verbal nods, etc., are also seen as agreement to the statement rather than an acknowledgement of understanding what has been said.'

It was also pointed out, that language differences can discriminate against black and ethnic minority candidates at the job interview stage:

> During interviews, including written tests, black candidates often do not always perform so well in the eyes of the white panels. This is because they are expected to speak and write the Queen's English. A black person may not say things in so much detail but rather concentrate upon practical details, putting things simply in order to get the message across.

Doyle and Paludi (1995) make the important point that the depiction of ethnic minority women and men speaking English in the media, is often racist. They refer to children's books about Puerto Ricans and Chicanos which often link a failure to speak English well with poverty. In films and television, they point out that the use of language characterisations such as stilted English suggest that ethnic minorities are less powerful and intelligent than white English-speaking characters and also help to sustain racial stereotyping.

A highly educated Asian woman director felt somewhat weary at not fitting into other people's fixed stereotypes:

> Most people I meet in business have this stereotype in their head of how an Asian woman should be and how she should speak. People therefore are often very surprised. I'm not sure what they expect but I think they expect you to be much more 'ethnic' – whatever that means. I find the private sector senior male managers have the most trouble. When I was in Saudia Arabia recently with my husband at a function, this man (white) said to us – 'I wouldn't have associated you two with our language – you speak such eloquent English – we never think of you as 'one of them'. What is 'one of them'?, I thought.

The English language treats both women and ethnic minorities in less than an equitable fashion. Doyle and Paludi (1995) emphasise the dominance of language formation by white males and how more effort should be made to avoid using discriminatory speech:

> Men – white men – have played the largest role in creating language, and their views of women have been translated far more fruitfully than many may wish to acknowledge. We live in a sexist and patriarchal society, and our language portrays these ideologies well. Learning to watch our language is a cliché most of us were taught as children. If avoiding offensive language is something we value, why 'then can we not watch our language even more closely lest it offend over half of the human race?

Indeed, the amazing callousness of white males' use of racist comments is illustrated by the following accounts described by two of the management interviewees:

> I recently attended a meeting with a few of my male colleagues (all white). At one point, one of them suddenly exclaimed, 'I think we have a problem here,

definitely a nigger in the wood pile!' I couldn't believe what I was hearing. What made it worse, was that nobody else seemed to even notice what he'd said. He certainly didn't. I made a point of saying I thought his comment was totally inappropriate. He looked embarrassed and apologised. Maybe next time, he'll think before he speaks.

Recently, one of our senior male (white) executives from head office addressed a group of employees who were predominantly black. The occasion was to enhance racial/equal opportunities within the company. He asked the audience a question and when a male black member of the ensemble spoke up with the answer, the executive yelled from the platform, 'well done, excellent answer – give that man a banana'. I almost fell off my chair, I just couldn't believe someone could say such a thing – particularly on such an occasion. He just didn't think.

Finally, many of the sample volunteered, without prompting, the fact that most white people they worked with would never talk to them about their race or make any reference to it – it was a taboo subject: 'People just seem to find it impossible to make any reference to your ethnic background. It's a taboo subject, even on training courses. While gender issues seem to have come out of the woodwork a bit more – racial issues certainly haven't.'

CONCLUSIONS

What is evident from the material reviewed in this chapter is that black and ethnic minority women managers' relationships in the workplace, particularly with whites, are often contaminated with issues surrounding both sexism and racism, racial taboos, negative stereotypes and cultural differences.

Dickens and Dickens (1991), assert that unlike white managers, 'black' managers have to develop strategies for dealing effectively with racist behaviour in order to perform their jobs well. These authors emphasise that both white and 'black' managers need to learn how to manage both racist and sexist behaviour in the workplace, as these are important techniques inherent in multicultural management. The problems are not associated with racist attitudes *per se*, rather it is the resulting *behaviour* of individuals acting out their racist beliefs that causes problems. Below are paraphrased the six key principles isolated by Dickens and Dickens (1991) that 'black' managers should adopt in order to manage racist behaviour that interferes with their effectiveness as professionals:

1. Understand that you must manage the racist behaviour of others in order to be successful and that you are not the only black manager to have to learn to do this.
2. Realise that you do not have to deal with this situation alone – ask others to share how they manage racist behaviour.

3. Allow yourself to recognise racist behaviour in action.
4. Take a risk and confront dysfunctional racist behaviour.
5. Understand the black–white dynamics that occur between individuals.
6. Apply effective techniques for managing racist behaviour by:
   - strategy;
   - controlling the behaviour of others;
   - controlling yourself;
   - using organisational norms and values;
   - using the communications network;
   - using the power of your boss;
   - using the power of your organisational position.

It should also be noted that these women managers' experiences of sexual harassment in the workplace are often quite different from their white female counterparts and these differences must be acknowledged. Marshall (1994) summarised this viewpoint aptly, when she wrote:

> Failure to recognise the different experiences of black women misrepresents not only our lives but also by implication those of white women. A full understanding of the construction of white female sexuality, necessitates an awareness of the construction of black female sexuality. It is not acceptable merely to add the experiences of black women to mainstream feminist analysis of sexuality. Instead, such research needs to be reconceptualised in order to examine the specific experiences of black women.

These types of relationship issues, whether they be dealing with sexuality, racism or communication differences, need to be brought out into the open and discussed in secure environments as part of multicultural management techniques. Thomas (1989) for example, proposes that these taboos and unspoken thoughts, ought to be safely expressed in meetings and workshops within organisations:

> This is a complex design and facilitation task and in my experience such encounters work only when black and white people participate in them together. We have only just begun to develop a social technology for confronting the racial taboos. But to be true to our pluralist values and to be socially responsible executives, we have no choice.

5

Occupational Stress and the Acquisition of Appropriate Management Skills

The racism and sexism I've had to endure leads to a lot of mental stress. I had to turn to a stress counsellor twice, due to stress at work.

The aim of this chapter is to discuss some of the issues related to the plight of black and ethnic minority women managers in terms of occupational stress and its effect on the individual, including the acquisition of appropriate management skills. Obviously, the theme of pressure flows throughout this book and both the bicultural role stressors and relationship pressures experienced by these women were more fully reviewed in the previous chapters. Having spent many years investigating occupational stress in female white managers, the aim was to ascertain whether the added dimension of race meant that these women managers were experiencing additional work stressors compared to their white female counterparts. Firstly, the literature pertaining to occupational stress and the white woman manager will be reviewed before concentrating specifically on those stressors more prominent for black and ethnic minority female managers.

OCCUPATIONAL STRESS AND WHITE FEMALE AND MALE MANAGERS

The costs of occupational stress for organisations is substantial. In America, Elkin and Rosch (1990) estimated that of the 550 million working days lost per year due to absenteeism, around 54% of these absences are stress-related in some way. According to Discoll and Cooper (1996), in the UK 360 million working days are lost annually through sickness at a cost to

Small sections of this chapter originally appeared in Davidson, M.J., Cooper C.L. and Baldini, V. (1995) Occupational Stress in Female and Male Graduate Managers – A Comparative Study. *Stress Management*, 11, 157–75; and also Davidson, M.J. (1997) Stress and The Black Woman Manager, in R. Burke (Ed) *Business and the Contemporary World*, New York: Wiley.

organisations of £8 billion each year. Similarly, it has been estimated by the UK Health and Safety Executive that around half of these lost days relate to stress-related absence (Discoll and Cooper, 1996).

Certain female-dominated jobs such as clinical technician, waitress and secretary, have been shown to be particularly stressful (Terbourg, 1985). While paid employment provides many positive benefits for women, for some, especially the working wife, the excessive pressure and scarcity of free time can adversely affect their ability to cope. In some cases, the result may be mental and physical illness such as headaches, anxiety, high blood pressure and depression. This, in turn can sometimes result in changed sleeping habits; decreased work performance, smoking, alcohol and drug abuse; occasional absenteeism; and poor personal relationships with colleagues (Davidson and Cooper, 1983, 1987, 1992; Devanna, 1987).

In particular, it is 'token women' working in non-traditional jobs, whether blue- or white-collar, who have been found to suffer most from stress related to discrimination and prejudice at work. Numerous studies have concluded that managerial and professional women experience unique sources of stress related to their minority status and gender, and that these stressors result in higher levels of overall occupational stress compared to their male counterparts. Devanna (1987) and Greenglass (1995) both found that professional women experience more headaches, more depression and more role conflict than men. Moreover, Greenglass (1990) reported that high role conflict in areas involving family and work roles were correlated with high Type A coronary-prone behaviour scores for professional women. Type A is the overt behavioural syndrome characterised by extremes of competitiveness, striving for achievement, aggressiveness, haste and feelings of being under pressure of time and under the challenge of responsibility.

Although coronary heart disease (CHD) is generally more prevalent in men than in women, some research findings are disturbing. For example, Haynes and Feinleib (1980) reanalysed prospective data drawn from the American Framingham Heart Study and discovered that working women did not have a significantly higher incidence of coronary heart disease than housewives and their rates were lower than for working men. However, they then analysed the data in terms of married, including divorced, widowed and separated, versus single working women and found a substantial increase in the incidence of heart disease among married women. The most revealing of all their results appeared when they compared married women with children against those without children. In this case, they found that 'amongst working women, the incidence of coronary heart disease rose as the number of children increased'. This was not the case, however, for women who were housewives. Indeed, that group showed a slight decrease with an increasing number of children. Couple these findings with the strong association between Type A behaviour and CHD, along with hypertension, and one could hypothesise that those female managers most at risk are those high Type A women who are married with children.

Moreover, Cooper *et al.* (1988) refer to a review of the research literature on marital adjustment in dual-career marriages, in which a University of Michigan team found that of the 13 important studies using a US national or regional sample, at least 11 indicated that marital adjustment was worse for dual-career wives than for non-working wives (Staines *at al.*, 1979).

To date, one of the largest UK studies investigating the occupational stressors and stress outcomes associated with being a female manager compared to her male counterpart was carried out by the author and Cary Cooper in the 1980s (Davidson and Cooper, 1982, 1983, 1986, 1987.) Qualitative data were obtained from in-depth interviews with a stratified, random sample of 60 female managers, with larger-scale questionnaire survey data collected on 696 female and 185 male managers. The results indicated that women managers experienced more external discriminatory-based pressures compared to male managers. The specific stressors which were isolated as being unique to female managers included:

- strains of coping with prejudice and sex stereotyping;
- overt and indirect discrimination from fellow employees;
- employers and the organisational structure and climate;
- lack of role models and feelings of isolation;
- burdens of coping with the role of the 'token woman'.

In the home and social arena, compared to male managers, women managers reported significantly higher pressure in respect to career and spouse/partner conflicts, career/home conflicts and career and marriage/child-bearing conflicts. Single women managers also faced higher pressures than their male counterparts in relation to feeling 'an oddity', being excluded from social/business events and career conflict over whether to start a family.

The major research approach to individual stress differences began with the work of Rosenman *et al.* (1966) in the early 1960s, and developed later showing a relationship between behavioural patterns and the prevalence of coronary heart disease (CHD). They found that individuals manifesting certain behavioural traits were significantly more at risk of CHD – these were referred to as the 'coronary-prone behaviour pattern Type A' as distinct from Type B (low risk CHD). Type A was found to be the overt behavioural syndrome or style of living characterised by 'extremes of competitiveness, striving for achievement, aggressiveness, haste, impatience, restlessness, hyper-alertness, explosiveness of speech, tenseness of facial musculature and feelings of being under pressure of time and under the challenge of responsibility'. It was suggested that 'people having this particular behavioural pattern were often so deeply involved and committed to their work that other aspects of their lives were relatively neglected'. While women managers had significantly higher Type A coronary-prone behaviour scores than men, there were few gender differences connected to coping strategies of the adoption of different management styles. Turning to stress manifestations, female managers reported that they experienced a far greater number of psychosomatic symptoms compared to men. Their total mean psychosomatic ill-health score was also significantly higher (Davidson and Cooper, 1982, 1983).

Cooper and Melhuish (1984) supplemented and reinforced some of the original findings of Davidson and Cooper (1987) by carrying out a longitudinal health and stress study on 311 senior male managers and 171 senior female managers. Several interesting findings emerged, which help further to explain previous work. First, when male executives seem to be at risk from stress-related illness, this tends to take the form of physical ill-health, whereas for female managers, it is more likely to develop into mental ill-health. Second, Type A behaviour is predictive of cardiovascular risk and poor physical and mental health for both male and female managers, but this is particularly true for women. Third, a significant predictor of adverse stress and health manifestations for women managers is 'responsibility for large numbers of people'. This may be due to the difficulty that female executives seem to face in delegating responsibility, as Davidson and Cooper (1983) found in their study. Fourth, it was found that male executives have higher stressor scores for more work factors than women in the following: 'responsibility for people', 'frequent promotions', 'frequent locations', 'more nights away from home on business' and 'overall stress at work'. On the other hand, these factors are not particularly strong predictors of ill-health, that is cardiovascular risk, physical or mental health, among men but are significant predictors for female managers. It could be that, although men find these job factors stressful, they have lived with them long enough to adapt, whereas women having only comparatively recently entered the management field, have less tolerance to these work stressors, even at low levels.

Similar findings were revealed in a recent UK study of 323 men managers and 51 women managers. Scase and Goffee (1989) reported that 84% of the male managers and 88% of the female managers claimed to work an average week in excess of 50 hours, due mainly to work overload and time pressures exacerbated by resource cutbacks. An increase in the length of the working week was particularly prominent in younger managers, especially women, and almost 40% of men and women reported frequent feelings of frustration. Scase and Goffee (1989) also confirmed previous findings that junior and middle managers are far more vulnerable to occupational stress compared to senior executives.

More recently, the levels of occupational stress in 126 female graduate managers occupying a range of managerial jobs throughout the UK were investigated (Davidson *et al.*, 1995). Although this study failed to find statistically significant differences between Type A scores between males and females, the results did reveal substantial adverse consequences of stress for management graduates, particularly in terms of mental and physical ill-health and job satisfaction. This trend became even worse when the sample of female management graduates was analysed. In fact, the study showed that little has changed in the past decade or so to help eliminate the extra sources of pressure suffered by female managers, and many of these results mirror those found in the early 1980s.

Female management graduates are still suffering significantly higher levels of mental and physical ill-health symptoms compared with their male counterparts, and are less satisfied with their jobs. They also reported significantly higher pressure scores on the main sources of job pressure categories i.e.

- factors intrinsic to the job;
- relationships with other people;
- career and achievement;
- organisational design and structure;
- home/work interface;
- gender factors, e.g. sexual harassment.

In particular, female middle and junior graduate managers seemed under much more pressure than their male colleagues, and even senior female graduate managers reported experiencing higher stressors stemming from discrimination and prejudice, i.e. the 'gender factor' (Davidson *et al.*, 1995).

OCCUPATIONAL STRESS AND THE BLACK AND ETHNIC MINORITY WOMAN MANAGER

Despite the fact that the proportion of minority group members in the total workforce in the UK and the USA is increasing, and projected to continue to do so, little research has examined work stress among minority employees (James, 1994; James, Lovato and Khoo, 1994).

While numerous cross-cultural studies conclude that white managerial women experience unique sources of stress related to their minority status and gender compared to their white male counterparts, American research confirms that black and ethnic minority managers (particularly women) are doubly disadvantaged in terms of upward mobility and high levels of work and have additional pressures (Bell, 1990; Greenhaus *et al.*, 1990)

Most Common Reported Work Stressors

Research investigating the main sources of stress intrinsic to the job that seem to affect white women managers have isolated:

- work overload;
- feeling undervalued, and hence not being given enough demanding work to do;
- 'being the boss';

- having to acquire male managerial skills;
- being assertive and confident;
- attending or being unable to attend training

(Davidson and Cooper, 1992)

When the 30 black and ethnic minority women managers we asked to reveal what they viewed as work stressors for them, similar sources of work stressors were isolated (see Table 5.1). The most commonly cited stressor was performance pressures followed by work overload/deadlines/time pressures, feeling undervalued/underutilised, feelings of powerlessness, needing to be qualified and delegation. However, what made these stressors *different* from those of their white female counterparts is that the sources of these stressors were often linked to the double bind i.e. sexism *and* racism.

Performance pressure has already been discussed in Chapter 3 and is typified once again in the following quotation: 'As a black woman manager I have to perform outstandingly – I have to justify my existence *far* more. Any mistakes would be remembered for a *long* time.' The pressure to work harder to prove themselves has also been inevitably linked to numerous studies finding that white women managers are frequently subjected to work overload and time pressures (Powell, 1988). Work overload can be seen as being either quantitative, because there is too much to do, or qualitative, because the work is too difficult, and can lead to a range of stress-related illnesses. French and Caplan (1970) found that managers with more phone calls, office visits and meetings per given unit of work time, smoked significantly more cigarettes than persons with fewer such engagements, and that smoking together with other stressors was a significant risk factor in coronary heart disease.

Margolis *et al.* (1974), in a large-scale study, found that job overload was associated with such stress-related symptoms as low work motivation, lowered self-esteem and escapist drinking. There are a large number of other studies which link overload with ill health and job dissatisfaction, but the important part here is that female managers, from all ethnic backgrounds, may be more at risk of overload than their male counterparts.

Table 5.1 shows that more than half of the interviewees reported stress due to feeling undervalued/underutilised (60%) and due to feelings of powerlessness (53%). Once again, both these stressors were linked particu-

Table 5.1   Most commonly reported work stressors

Sexism and racism issues	%	(N)
Work overload/deadlines/time pressures	63.3	(19)
Performance pressure	83.3	(25)
Feeling undervalued/underutilised	60.0	(18)
Feelings of powerlessness	53.3	(16)
Qualifications	33.3	(10)
Delegation	13.3	(4)

larly to racism combined with gender issues. An Afro-Caribbean woman working in the health service commented:

> People should have realised before that I could easily have done this job but they didn't give me a chance until now. I find it very frustrating when they do not appear to value my qualities and experience.
>
> I often do feel powerless and disillusioned because racist attitudes appear so ingrained.

Another Indian female executive went on to describe her feelings of powerlessness by saying: 'I feel that people do not listen to what you say. I often have to compromise with people and keep quiet. As a black woman – you are the one voice.'

Feeling undervalued was also often linked to low pay and an Indian woman in personnel described her absolute disillusionment by saying:

> I feel totally undervalued and my pay is far too low. They don't make use of my psychometric skills, training or my contacts. I use them, but for my benefit.
>
> I feel utterly powerless to change anything. It's like banging your head against a brick wall. After maternity leave, I became even more powerless and I certainly link it to both my sex and the colour of my skin.

A third of the interviewees quoted the stressors associated with needing to be more qualified. However, as previously discussed in Chapter 2, as a sample these women were highly qualified and the stress was linked often to feeling they had to be three times better qualified than their white counterparts. A few women felt the qualifications they had gained, such as MBA's, were a double-edged sword – they were now in danger of being overqualified! This was felt to be a lose–lose situation: 'I initially felt I needed to be better qualified than my white peers in order to get on. However, now people say to me I'm overqualified. This is a common problem for black women in my position.'

The final most commonly reported stressor was linked to delegation. In previous research concentrating on white women managers, it has been suggested that 'credibility testing' pressure, combined with feelings of 'being exceptional' or isolated, may induce blocks regarding delegation. Obviously, inability to delegate work can cause excessive overload. Certainly, black and ethnic minority women managers reported similar issues but these were also sometimes combined with racial as well as gender issues:

> While I think I use a good delegation style and am autonomous and demand accountability, I feel there are cultural issues which can be problematic for me. I *ask* people to do things, but I *expect* them to do it. Sometimes I feel there is a misunderstanding and there are times when in the white culture one would 'tell' rather than 'request'.

When the sample were asked to state which particular stressors they found *most* stressful, many were again linked to racial and gender factors. It can be

Table 5.2   Which particular stressors do you find most stressful? (in order of repeated frequency)

Stressors related to sexism and racism issues
★ Work overload/time pressures/deadline
★ Performance pressure due to colour
★ Home/work conflicts, including guilt re being working mother
Job insecurity
★ Coping with racism, and little support
Paperwork
★ Isolation – no other black females
★ Lack of support, especially from manager
Lack of role clarity
★ Pressure from higher management
★ Accused by other blacks of having 'sold out' by working for an all white organisation
★ Taking racist subordinate to Industrial Tribunal and being victimised
★ Threatened white female boss
Lack of funding
★ Reaching the glass ceiling
Problems with manufacturing process
★ Dealing with Asian male colleagues
The telephone
★ Tokenism due to colour
★ Having more stress than white colleagues
Bureaucracy

seen from Table 5.2 that work overload and performance pressure reared their ugly heads as leading major stressors, followed by home/work conflicts (see Chapter 2). Once more, it is interesting to note that unlike many white female managers, many of the problem areas for these female managers are strongly associated with both racial and gender prejudice and discrimination, e.g. performance pressure due to colour, coping with racism or isolation. American researchers such as Frone *et al.* (1990) and James *et al.* (1994) have found that perceived prejudice and discrimination in Euro-American organisations were unique sources of stress for ethnic minority workers above and beyond other work stressors. James (1994) and James *et al.* (1994) very much emphasise the importance of social identity and minority worker's health and view social identities as an important source of stress and having an impact on stress coping ability:

> According to this theory, a desire to maintain a positive sense of identity – a sense of being held in esteem – is seen as a major force driving individuals' cognitions, emotions and behaviours. Individual–ingroup and ingroup–outgroup relations are related, according to Tajfel and Turner, because much of an individual's ability to maintain a positive sense of esteem depends on ingroup–outgroup comparisons.

Because group memberships contribute substantially to identity and a sense of esteem, they are capable of broad influence. Race is a membership category that has strong chronic implications for social identity in the United States for historical, cultural, and social-structure reasons (Allport, 1954; Tajfel and Turner, 1979). Because most minority individuals work for majority-dominated companies, the racial component of identity also becomes acutely prominent by way of contrast (James and Khoo, 1991; Pettigrew and Martin, 1987). Racial identity can create social stressors for minority workers and lower their resistance to stress.

(James *et al.*, 1994, p. 384)

James *et al.* (1994) have pinpointed six variables involved in social identity processes in organisations which have been previously correlated with minority workers' health. These include individual expressiveness (see Chapter 4), levels of perceived prejudice and discrimination experienced on the job, perceived differences in values between minority and majority organisation members addressed separately for supervisors and for peers (see relationship issues in Chapter 4) and levels of self- and collective, ethnic-group-based esteem. Obviously, threads of these variables have been interwoven throughout this book. However, good self-esteem is certainly linked with a strong belief in self and good self-confidence. It was found that 60% of the interviewees were satisfied with their feelings of confidence and over three-quarters with their independence. This black and ethnic minority female staff-sufficiency-independence seems to substantiate previous American research. Epstein (1973) for example, found black and ethnic minority women professionals had acquired a sense of confidence in their competence and abilities and proposed that this was probably reinforced as they overcame each obstacle on the way to the top. Simpson (1984) on the other hand, refers to Watson's (1974) thesis of ego formation of black and ethnic minority women, drawn upon theories based on the process of symbolic interaction. This assumes that the self-concept, how one feels about oneself, is a flexible, structural process which is not static and rather than being a passive recipient, the woman can be active in shaping her self-image:

Traditional approaches to the development of the self-concept assume that the individual is socialised into a society. The individual develops a picture of self consistent with the socialisation process. But black women are not valued by this society (Davis, 1973; 1989) and therefore consciously reject this inferior image of themselves by assuming a more active role in the development of their self-concept. Under the conditions of negative social and inferior caste status, individuals are likely to assume a very active role with regard to 'selves'; this action is likely to take the form of 'self' creation, rather than 'self defense', and that response evocation will be designed to promote new self images rather than maintain old ones.

(Watson, 1974, cited by Simpson, 1984)

Interestingly, for the 40% of women manager interviewees who felt they lacked confidence, this was blamed either on lack of qualifications, their individual personality and/or their colour i.e. 'self defense' rather than 'self' creation:

I've always been under confident and I believe that this is due in part to me being black. My lack of confidence affects everything that I do and I would have had more self confidence if I were white. I often worry about what my staff think of my performance.

Lack of confidence was also associated with not being assertive enough, particularly with other white employers/ees:

I do lack confidence and I have to work in a predominantly white, male group. I'm not sure why – perhaps its about not being taken seriously enough. I feel I often make obvious statements and then I think I'm wasting their time. So, if I've got something to say, I like to be brief. Then I realise afterwards, I've been too brief!

As a result of lacking confidence (due to lack of qualifications), I'm not assertive enough, The white male and female managers are more confident than myself. This has been my downfall. People have just taken advantage. I should have done a lot of things early on to assert myself. People wouldn't have liked it, but it's what they expect and I wouldn't be having all this trouble now.

MANIFESTATIONS OF STRESS

The vast majority, 83%, of black and ethnic minority women managers reported negative stress manifestations, psychological, physical and behavioural. When probed as to whether these stress reactions were instigated by negative factors linked to race, gender and/or other, stressors linked to racial issues were the most prominent:

At the probation services, the racism wore me down. Nobody would take action. I was on my own and I therefore found it very difficult to cope.

The racism and sexism I've had to endure leads to a lot of mental stress. I had to turn to a stress counsellor twice, due to stress at work.

Table 5.3 highlights the most commonly reported symptoms of stress manifestations in order of reported frequency with the most prominent being:

- depression/stress/anxiety;
- job dissatisfaction;
- exhaustion;
- sleeping problems and physical ill-health.

One of the few comparative studies investigating occupational stress, social support and depression among black and ethnic minority (N = 100) and white (N = 100) American professional-managerial women was carried out by Snapp (1992). She found that for both 'black' and white women, of the occupational stressors, only trouble with boss or subordinates was significantly related to levels of depression. Moreover, race was a significant predictor of both levels of social support and occupational stress. The black and ethnic minority women reported lower levels of co-worker support, workload, and trouble with subordinates or boss than the white women. Compared to middle class 'black' women, white women and 'black' women from working class backgrounds reported lower levels of family support (Snapp, 1992). James *et al.* (1994) also found that relations with supervisors affect minority workers circumstances, including their health, more than relations with non-minority peers.

The range of symptoms that black and ethnic minority women managers suffered is revealed by some of the following interview vignettes:

> Poor relationships with white directors and black staff led to my depression. I went to the doctor because I was suicidal. He offered me tranquillizers, but I refused. I had help from my friends and the Samaritans. I have more or less come out of it now.

> The racism in my last job led to loss of self-esteem and lack of confidence as well as depression and mild paranoia. Eventually, I left the job.

> I do not let racism get to me psychologically anymore. I once worked in a hospital for 10 weeks, where the racism was so appalling that I left. I could not stand it. I complained, but nothing was done.

> A big part of my job was anti-racist training and it was a very stressful 3 years. You are the problem up there, you are the only voice. I felt it was my sole responsibility. I have burnt out – I'm really tired – I took 4 weeks off work and my manager had to pace out what I had to do once I returned.

> I often feel really tired – tired all the time – even when I just wake up.

> My sleeping pattern has been affected – but I have learned to cope with stress better in the last 6 months. At first I felt I needed to achieve and demonstrate that I could cope as well as my white male colleagues – they were all married with wives at home. They had a strong social support network, whereas I

Table 5.3 Negative psychosocial and health outcomes related to sexism and racism at work

Most common report symptoms in order of reported frequency

 1. Depression/stress/anxiety
 2. Job dissatisfaction
 3. Exhaustion/tiredness
 4. Difficulty in sleeping
 5. Physical ill-health, e.g. skin disease, breast cancer
 6. Quitting the job
 7. Loss of confidence
 8. Impaired job performance
 9. Suicidal thoughts
10. Unable to relax
11. Dampened career aspirations
12. Taking time off work
13. Anger/frustration

Note: 83.3% (N = 25) reported negative effects with racism commonly being major cause.

worked all day and went home alone. My boss would use kids as an excuse but I felt I had as many problems. I now worry if I have a family – how I will cope. I know I will have to go back to work straight away after having children – you're perceived here as being less capable if you take a break.

I get tired fighting to break through all the time. I've hit my glass ceiling but I *will* get through it. If you've been shortlisted, as I have for a £100,000 a year job, then you're worth £100,000 – I know that.

I get tired – I find it sometimes difficult to sleep and wake up in the middle of the night and work. I tend to withhold tension – I have no one to take it out on, I can't take it out on my child. I tend to scream out at the boss sometimes. I have breast cancer at the moment – it could have been due to pressure – the continual build up of resentment over the years – I just couldn't let the tensions out.

I have the skin disease psoriasis which is supposedly due to stress. It does get worse if the pressure increases at work.

The physical side of stress for me is that I'm overweight and I don't like it at 33. I look like I'm 43 and feel like 53! I'm short tempered and have more headaches. I resent not having more time for myself, even if its only 10 minutes in the day.

Other than anger – I do not allow stress to have negative effects. I have a sense of being right with myself, as I have a base – a home in Jamaica. People born here don't have those roots, that kind of base – the ground is more level because of it, but there are still a lot of hills.

MANAGERIAL SKILLS AND STYLE

Another potential source of stress on white female managers has been mentioned in the research literature, and involves the pressure to adopt male managerial attributes and skills, such as being more assertive, confident, decisive and delegatory.

Hirsh and Jackson (1989) refer to an earlier study (Hirsh and Bevan, 1988) which found that criteria for management positions, particularly at senior level, were not only very 'male' but also vague. According to Hirsh and Jackson (1989):

They highlight the dominant, assertive, decisive aspects of behaviour and downplay the team and supportive behaviours which are perhaps more readily identified in women. These team behaviours are seen as increasingly important for management. Barham *et al.* (1988) portrays the future manager as less concerned with giving instructions and controlling subordinates and more concerned with maintaining a network of relationships across the organisation and with those outside, such as customers. The criteria used to assess managers may discriminate against women, but may also be using a model of management which is no longer appropriate for the work that managers do.

Researchers such as Rosener (1990) have reaffirmed that the traditional leadership style in organisations has been the male command-and-control style, known as 'Transactional Leadership Style'. This involves a series of transactions with subordinates exchanging rewards for services or punishment for inadequate performance. Transactional leadership style is commonly linked to male managers and is more likely to use power from organisational position and formal authority. Conversely, Rosener (1990) asserts that women are more likely to describe themselves in ways which characterise 'Transformational Leadership'. This style encourages subordinates to transform their self interest into interest of the group through concern for a broader goal. Consequently, this interactive leadership style encourages participation and ascribes power to personal characteristics such as interpersonal skills, hard work or charisma rather than from organisational stature (Wilson, 1995).

Recently, Rosener's theories have been confirmed by an American study carried out by Bass *et al.* (1996), which showed that women seemed to be at least, if not more, transformational than men, and appeared to be perceived as practising less passive management-by-exception and *laissez-faire* leadership, than men. In addition, they found that generally, women leaders were not perceived all that differently from their male counterparts.

Dissatisfaction with training and inadequate training has also been shown to be a common complaint from female managers and is undoubtedly linked to the acquisition of appropriate management skills. Indeed, many women in the lower levels of management in the UK lag behind their male counterparts when it comes to the provision of training, due to a mixture of lack of opportunities and discrimination (Davidson and Cooper, 1992). Half of the black interviewees were dissatisfied with the training opportunities and experiences they had had. For some who voiced satisfaction, it was because of their own initiatives and self financing: 'I am now satisfied with my training but that's because I've carefully chosen the courses myself and in 90% of cases, paid for them myself.'

When the interviewees were questioned as to whether, like their white female counterparts (see Davidson and Cooper, 1992), they like 'being the boss', over three-quarters said 'yes'. Where there were dilemmas voiced about 'being the boss', these were sometimes linked with cultural, racial issues:

> While I like being the boss – I don't like the total responsibility as I'm always open to attack and criticism in the type of job I do (Policy Manager). As a black person, I feel more likely to be targeted.

> I like being the boss, but I do have difficulty with conflict. I think that's a cultural issue, being Indian. When I was 25, I was asked to manage a 55-year-old female nurse. She was very difficult and that created problems. I've since done a lot of self development and I therefore am beginning to become more at ease with my role as manager.

Current research suggests that today, the majority of middle, middle-upper and senior white female managers have benefited from both familiarity with their role of manager, and more often than not, favourable family background environments, and have learned *not* to fear success (Davidson and Cooper, 1992). Moreover, based on the interview data collected from the 30 black and ethnic minority female managers, there was little if any evidence of this 'fear of success syndrome' originally proposed by Horner (1972), i.e. women having difficulty in competitive situations with men because they feel that if they succeed, there will be negative consequences. The sample of women managers enjoyed being the boss and were just as ambitious, if not more so, than their white male and female counterparts.

Fear of success has also been linked with *locus* of control and some theorists have stated that women who choose traditional, female dominated careers have an external *locus* of control as opposed to those who opt for non-traditional careers, such as management, and have an internal *locus* of control. Evans and Herr (1991) suggest that the perception of sexism and racism in the workplace has a negative effect on a woman's belief in her ability to influence the world around her. Hence, they propose that African-American women appear to aspire to careers which will have the minimum exposure to racism and sexism and consequently, those traditionally dominated by women. According to Evans and Herr (1991):

> Savage, Stearns and Friedman (1979) observed that African American women who were externally influenced expressed more fear of success imagery, because they were more concerned with societal expectations. Savage *et al.* indicated that fear of success imagery may be a function of internalised racial and sex stereotyping. When this internalisation process is complete, the woman feels that she must give up to what is now her own view of what she can and cannot do.

It was evident from the responses from black and ethnic minority female managers throughout the interviews, that the majority had high internal *loci* of control and certainly did not fear success. Not only had they chosen male dominated occupations, but had often entered jobs where no black or ethnic minority person, male or female, had ever gone.

When we asked the black and ethnic minority women managers whether they thought they managed differently from their white male and female colleagues, 80% believed they did. What was interesting in these replies was that while the majority described using a more 'Transformational Leadership' style similar to their white female colleagues, many also linked their different style to cultural differences:

> Being a woman, I think I work in a different way. I may also react differently as an Asian woman to certain situations. My female white colleague, for example, would approach Elders (Asian men) on a committee differently to me due to my cultural background. My eye contact, even with white men is very different to hers.

I feel my style is more inclusive – I'm more sensitive to atmosphere. I expect a lot from people who work for me. I have a more personal style – a more 'caring' style. When I work at a regional level, I have to learn to stay sane. I have to cope with an 'adoration complex' from white men – they don't challenge you enough. They listen, but expect you to cope alone.

I think I do manage differently and it's due both to my gender and my colour. I have to adapt depending on the job and who I'm talking to. I feel I can't be me sometimes – I have to carefully choose my approach each time. Being 'big', 'black' and 'female' – people presume often I'm going to be aggressive.

I feel I do manage differently from my white colleagues. I'm always concerned about people's feelings and I manage in a way in order to decrease conflict. I try and have a wider perspective of what is going on. As a black person – you can't *ever* overlook how people react to you and what they expect from you.

To date, there has been little in-depth research investigating gender *and* racial differences in the ways individuals 'manage'. Clearly, this is an area in management and leadership styles which requires further research. One should also consider Wilson's (1995) suggestion that we might decide to give up organisations based on hierarchy and consequently surrender the use of concepts such as leader and subordinate. She refers to some literature now promoting 'flatter' less hierarchial forms or organisation which emphasise autonomy, collaboration and flexibility.

CONCLUSIONS

The evidence presented in this chapter suggests that while white men and white women managers often share common stressors, black and ethnic minority managerial women experience unique sources of stress related to their minority status and gender. However, the evidence from the data analysed from the 30 black and ethnic minority female management interviewees, supports previous American findings that these particular women managers in the UK are often doubly disadvantaged and have to cope with additional stressors linked to both gender and racial issues. The most commonly cited pressures often combine elements of both sexism and racism and included performance pressures, work overload/deadlines/time pressures, feeling undervalued/underutilised, feelings of powerlessness, and a need for qualifications. Furthermore, more than 80% of the sample reported negative psychosocial and health outcomes which were related to sexism and racism at work – racism being the most often quoted as being the major cause. Hence, this lends further support for the urgent need for organisational and policy changes to help relieve and eliminate some of these major stressors.

6

Career Development: Racism and Sexism – The Double Bind

The person in my job before me was a white male and he was on three salary levels higher than me! I haven't questioned it yet – once I prove myself, I certainly will. If I'd been a white female, I think I'd be two grades higher than I am now. If I were a white male, I'd certainly be further up the management chain.

This chapter will address issues involved in the black and ethnic minority women managers' limited career prospects and promotion, as well as the career phases and potential barriers. It will continue to explore the double bind of racism and sexism which according to Evans and Herr (1991) are similar processes that operate independently but produce an additive effect. Indeed, according to Evans and Herr, African-American women face more discrimination than 'black' men or white women when the combined effects of racism and sexism in the workplace are taken into account cumulatively.

A number of large scale American surveys of male and female managers from different ethnic groups have illustrated that compared to white managers, black and ethnic minorities often:

- received lower salaries;
- felt less accepted in their organisations;
- perceived themselves as having less discretion in their jobs;
- received lower ratings from their supervisors on their job performance and promotion prospects;
- felt their career prospects were more limited;
- were more likely to have reached career plateaux;
- experienced lower levels of career satisfaction.

(Greenhaus *et al.*, 1990)

In addition, one survey revealed that black and ethnic minority applicants for a job would be less likely to be selected over a competing white if both were equally qualified (Cox, 1990).

Before examining these findings and related issues more fully, the foundations of career development phases for black and ethnic minority managers need to be explored, and have been appropriately formulated by Dickens and Dickens (1991).

FOUR-PHASE DEVELOPMENTAL MODEL

In their book *The Black Manager*, Dickens and Dickens (1991) presented a four-phase developmental model as a guide to the career movements of 'blacks in large white corporate settings'. This model, presented in Figure 6.1, was based on their research project investigating the experiences of African-American managers. Although their sample was predominantly male African-American managers, the authors propose that the model presented in Figure 6.1 is also applicable to men and women from both African-American and other ethnic minority groups.

According to Dickens and Dickens (1991) this is a close-looped repeating

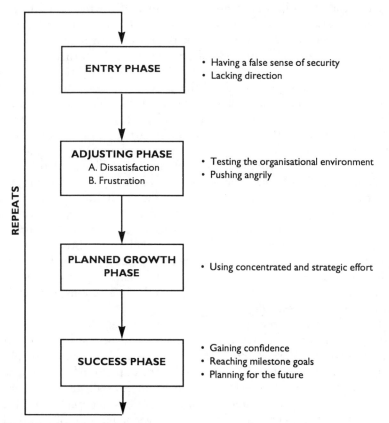

Figure 6.1 The four-phase development model

Source: Excerpted by permission of the publisher from *The Black Manager, Revised Version,* by F. Dickens et al., © 1991, AMACOM, a division of American Management Association, all rights reserved.

model, as once individuals reach the Success Phase, a new cycle commences with a major job change or reassignment to another organisation. They propose that it takes a shorter time period to traverse the cycle in subsequent job changes, each time a cycle is complete.

During the Entry Phase, 'black' managers tend to have unrealistic expectations about both the people they work with and the quality of their jobs. Once the reality of the uniqueness of their situation hits them, this is the crunch time when eventually they are propelled either 'out of the door or onto the next stage of development'. In the Adjusting Phase 'black' managers begin to acknowledge that the organisational system is presenting them with the same barriers that exist in society and that they are being faced with additional career obstacles not faced by their white counterparts. Whites in the organisation are often perceived as 'the enemy' and this is the phase whereby the stresses linked to blocked career progression begin to intensify.

Dickens and Dickens (1991) detail numerous strategies in order to progress from the Adjusting Phase to the Planned Growth Phase. However, this transgression is greatly facilitated if the 'black' manager begins to accept that when working with whites, there will always be a racial component 'that must be dealt with effectively if job performance is to be maximised'. Black managers at this stage have to stop fighting against this fact and need to accept that one of the prices of success is to spend extra energy on planning and managing these black–white interactions, i.e. managing racism effectively. During the Planned Growth Phase, Dickens and Dickens propose that 'black' managers start to substitute their resentment towards whites and acknowledge that most whites are ignorant about how 'blacks' have to cope with racism in organisations. At this phase, 'black' managers will isolate the bigots, act accordingly and concentrate on utilising other whites as resources for more than technical matters. In addition to managing various white interactions more effectively, this is a phase when 'black' managers use other black resources such as black network groups, black role models, black peers, etc. This is also a time when successful 'black' managers will realise they must be flexible in their management style and behaviour and 'seek whatever personal style best facilitates the most effective, and profitable interactions with others' (Dickens and Dickens, 1991).

Once 'black' managers reach the Success Phase, they have learnt to develop behaviours which work well and discard those that proved dysfunctional. However, Dickens and Dickens emphasise that even at this phase, 'black' managers still view themselves as having to perform better and maintain a higher level of interpersonal and behavioural skills than white males do. They have learned to sublimate their emotions and anger and rage is now redirected and energised into constructive acquisition of appropriate strategic skills. Nevertheless, an important factor at this phase is that 'black' managers must remain aware of prejudiced behaviour and respond selectively if it threatens their progression or survival. In addition, these authors found that most successful 'black' managers believed their success was also due to their being continually aware of how their blackness impacted on the white organisation: 'It is not too strong a statement to say that forgetting these factors is tantamount to a *loss of survival instincts*. Black managers who forget may find themselves quite easily brushed aside and forgotten' (Dickens and Dickens, 1991).

In the sample of British black and ethnic minority female interviewees, it was evident that these managers were at different phases of Dickens and Dickens (1991) career progression model. Certainly those female managerial interviewees who were in the Entry and Adjustment Phases were suffering the highest levels of stress. This was aptly illustrated by Chapter 1's opening vignette describing experiences of the junior manager 'Colette', whose energies finally became exhausted in her fight against racism and sexism, and who eventually chose to 'propel *herself* through the door'. While Dickens and Dickens model of 'black' managerial career development is certainly applicable to black and ethnic minority female managers, it is predominantly a male model and the following career development issues concerning both racism *and* sexism, including pay, need also to be discussed more fully.

PAY

In the European Union countries, while gender pay gaps persist in every member state, the size of the gap varies not only by country but also between manual and non-manual jobs (Davidson, 1996). Women in manual jobs earn between 67% and 84% of men's average pay. The ratio is the highest in Denmark, Italy and Greece where it ranges from 79% to 84%, and lowest in the UK, Luxembourg and Ireland where it stands between 67% and 70%. The difference in earnings between male and female non-manual workers is even wider. Women in non-manual work receive less than two-thirds of men's average pay in all countries except four, Germany, France, Greece and Portugal (Rubery, Fagan and Grimshaw, 1994). In the UK in 1995, female earnings per week, as a percentage of male earnings, were 72% (New Earnings Survey, 1996). As far as white female managers are concerned, they are, on average, poorly paid compared to male managers in Europe, the USA and Australia (Davidson and Burke, 1994; Davidson, 1996). A recent UK National Management Survey (Institute of Management and Remuneration Economics, 1996) found that the average female manager earned £30,569 compared to £34,855 per annum earned by the average male manager. Even at Director level, the average female in 1996 earned £71,638 compared to her male colleagues who earned £88,390. A recent large scale study investigating the gender gap in career success of men and women in the British labour force revealed that although factors such as structural features of the organisations, labour market economic forces, career choices, demographic characteristics, job-relevant human capital attributes and personality characteristics explained a large amount of variance in career success, over 55% of the gender gap in career success was attributed to sex discrimination (Melamed, 1995).

Bhavnani (1994) asserts that despite the lack of national data on black women's pay, the evidence suggests a pay differential between black and ethnic minority and white women. She refers to a 1986 London Living Standards Survey which illustrated that the hourly differential between 'black' and white women could be as great as 23%. American research also parallels these findings and African-Americans continue to be the most underemployed and underpaid adults (Evans and Herr, 1991). In 1987, the average American black family earned $18,000 a year which represented 56% of the average white family income of $32,270.

The limited studies assessing the pay of black and ethnic minority women managers and professionals, also highlight pay differentials between their white and black and ethnic minority male counterparts. Essed (1991) compared the job opportunities for highly educated American 'black' women with those of 'black' men, and concluded that 'black' women are more likely to end up in the lower paying jobs. In Williams' (1989) study of American college 'black' administrators, a third of the female respondents did not believe they were currently receiving pay equal to that of their male counterparts and another third were unsure

More than half (16) of the women managers interviewed maintained they were being paid less than their white counterparts. One Indian Personnel Officer said: 'Somebody who I manage who is female and white, is on a higher rate of pay than me. I certainly believe that if I were white, I would be earning more than I am now.' Another female Caribbean Director complained: 'I haven't had a pay rise in four years. The last time I delivered a project I was given a pay cut! I felt I was expected to beg for it – but I didn't.' It should also be noted that despite the fact that five women were part-time/job share one-third of the sample were in senior management jobs, compared to around 2–3% of all female managers, who are predominantly white. The average salary was £26,500 per annum which compared to £28,642 per year earned by the average female manager in the UK in 1995, the year in which the interviews took place (Institute of Management and Remuneration Economics, 1995).

When each of the women managers was asked whether they thought they would be doing a different job with higher pay and status if they had been born a white woman, more than half (19) believed they would. An even higher 80% (24) believed they'd be in a more highly paid, higher status position if they'd been born a white man. One Afro-Caribbean female manager exclaimed: 'I always say to my boyfriend – if I could be blonde for a day – I'd be rich.' Another interviewee working in the public sector commented:

As a white woman, I would expect to be at a higher level and with a higher salary in this organisation. When I joined this department, I met a number of white women who were at my level and are now earning £5,000 more than me. I feel I have the same talents as them and believe I do the job better than those above me.

If on the other hand, I was an Indian male, I'd be applying for jobs at much higher grades. I wouldn't have the responsibilities that I have in my personal life. I must admit though, that most of the black male managers have been moved or deployed. What annoys me, is that they let them get their MBAs – though they didn't use them – whereas I was always refused when I applied to do an MBA. Certainly if I were a white male, I'd be on a lot more pay and have a much better job.

A senior female African executive in the private sector described even more overt racial discriminatory practices:

The person in my job before me was a white male and he was on three salary levels higher than me! I haven't questioned it yet – once I prove myself, I certainly will. If I'd been a white female, I think I'd be two grades higher than I am now. If I were a white male, I'd certainly be further up the management chain – I think I would have done a lot better education wise and had much better opportunities. When I was a clerical clerk, I had white male colleagues who were promoted well before me. For every one step up I have taken, I've had to prove myself three times more compared to them.

While 57% of the interviewees believed they faced blocked promotion and career progression, it is also worth mentioning that without prompting, a fifth of the sample volunteered that they believed their black and ethnic minority male counterparts were subjected to even more discrimination and prejudice than they were. Common observations on this subject include:

As a black male, I don't think I would have done so well. Black men have a rotten deal and a black man would have had to be very lucky to get where I am.

I think it's definitely harder for black males. I think they're seen more of a threat to the organisation. There's certainly a glass ceiling for them.

I know of black male colleagues who are paid less and face even more discrimination during job applications than black women. For example, a black male colleague who provides training for ethnic trainees is only paid £16,000 per year even though he manages more than 80 people!

GETTING THE JOB

At the Entry Phase of career progression, half of the interviewees described incidences in the past in which they strongly believed that racial discrimination was the main reason for them not getting a particular job or promotion. A senior manager in the health services recounted:

There have been two instances where I applied for a job in a hospital, but a white female candidate who was less qualified and experienced than myself got the job. In addition, whilst her interview lasted ten minutes, mine lasted three quarters of an hour. I also went for a nursing officer post, but a white female internal candidate got the post. Again, she was less qualified than me. I asked for a post-interview meeting, but the panel seemed unable to articulate why I had not got the job. I later learned that one of the panel did not want a black manager.

Another senior executive in the private sector who had had a short career break, also felt her age combined with her colour and sex, had contributed towards discrimination at the job applicant stage:

Being black, female and older has prevented me from getting jobs in the past. It took me a long time after my break – a further year, to get the job I have now. I went for one in the social sciences. The interviewer looked shocked when he saw me. He was concerned about how I would deal with white, middle-class clients. They rejected me for inappropriate reasons. For example, they said that I did not know enough about job descriptions, but they hadn't even asked me about this during my interview!

This type of racial discrimination, while acknowledged, was often hard to come to terms with as typified by the following comment: 'Certainly I have not got jobs in the past because of the colour of my skin. At first you deny it to yourself and you can't believe it – but later, you realise it's the case.'

A number of the interviewees had successfully combated this type of job interview discrimination by asserting their strong self-esteem in relation to their own job performance abilities, combined with the assumption that they need to be better at the job than their white counterparts:

I've never not got a job that I've been interviewed for. I make sure I'm always that much better than the others. Black people have to be *much better* applicants, in order to get the job in the first place.

The first job I applied for, I didn't get as it was clearly a white managerial role – a training tutor. When I refused to be rejected and insisted they should give me the job, they said 'OK – have a go, but we'll be here to pick up the pieces.' They obviously expected me to fail – but I didn't. When I trained for interviewing skills, the message that came across to me was they thought it was not the 'done thing' for a black woman to do.

JOB GHETTOISATION AND BLOCKED CAREER PROGRESSION

As previously discussed in Chapter 1, the job of management is also subjected to gender segregation with the majority of women managers concentrated in personnel and marketing (Institute of Management and Remuneration Economics, 1996). Bhavnani (1994) has highlighted that horizontal and vertical segregation are both racialised and gendered.

Certainly, black and ethnic minority women managers and professionals are occupationally segregated. 'Black' doctors for example, tend to be concentrated in the more unpopular specialities, and have had inferior training opportunities. Both American and Dutch research has found that black and ethnic minority women in the higher skilled jobs are often steered into 'ethnic' work (Essed, 1991). In the social services, Bhavnani (1994) suggests that there is more and more evidence that 'black' British women are working with predominantly 'black' clients and mainly in 'specialist' areas, i.e. being racially ghettoised:

> These included the appointment of black social workers for their cultural and linguistic skills who then become isolated in a hostile and unsupportive workforce; the marginalisation of 'race' equality advisers; the compartmentalisation of issues of 'race' and gender and the lack of emphasis on the relationship *between* various groups employed by local authorities.
>
> (Bhavnani, 1994)

A proportion of the interview sample were indeed 'ghettoised' into 'black' jobs although this had been by choice, particularly those related to equal opportunities and race relations. Even so, the majority of those women voiced concern about the career entrapment risks linked to this type of ghettoisation. For example, one race relations manager asserted: 'People have stereotypes about people (particularly black people) in "Race" or "Women's Units" and often think that we can't transfer our skills to other areas.' Indeed, one Equal Opportunities Manager we spoke to, had made a conscious decision to limit her time in that particular job in order to protect herself from this type of token ghettoisation and its possible career stagnation. As she explained:

> I think my brain is being underutilised but the colour of my face *is* being utilised. It will be an obstacle to me if I stay in the Equal Opportunity role too long – especially with my black face. I plan to give myself 18 months then I'll get out. Otherwise, I'll remain pigeonholed as the 'black EO female face' – forever!

CAREER PROSPECTS COMPARED TO WHITE MANAGERIAL COLLEAGUES

An American survey by Greenhaus, Parasuraman and Wormley (1990) investigated relationships among race, organisational experiences, job performance evaluations, and career outcomes for 828 black and ethnic minority and white managers (male and female) from three organisations. When asked to compare themselves with white managers, the interview sample responded almost identically to their 'black' American managerial counterparts. The majority of the sample of British black and ethnic minority women managers interviewed felt they were less accepted in the organisation (70%) and were more likely to have reached a career plateau (60%). In addition, half believed they received lower ratings from their supervisors on job performance and promotability compared to their white colleagues. However, only 40% believed that they were experiencing lower levels of career satisfaction.

Overall, the women manager interviewees felt at a disadvantage compared to their white colleagues in terms of career prospects, recognition and feeling valued by their bosses. In the study of female African-American College Administrators, Williams (1989) emphasised the importance of recognition for these women:

> Those who felt they got some or a great deal of recognition perceive themselves as being on the administration team. Self-perception can sometimes affect the job done. A person who feels good efforts are not acknowledged may not work as diligently on subsequent assignments, or she may begin to be perceived and treated differently by her administrative peers.
>
> (Williams, 1989)

In the USA, Dickens and Dickens (1991) note that 'blacks' and other ethnic minorities are leaving corporations in greater numbers than they have in the past two decades. These authors stress the importance for 'black' managers to plan their careers early to help eliminate and buffer some of the additional career progression barriers they face due to their colour. In the words of Dickens and Dickens (1991):

> Career planning helps to:
> * Compensate for lack of black role models
> * Reduce the effects of racism and sexism which prevent blacks and women from being able to take advantage of available opportunities
> * Manage the white fear of blacks
> * Reduce subjectivity in evaluations and increase objectivity
> * Reduce or eliminate low trust among racial groups by removing doubt so trust is no longer an issue
> * Raise blacks awareness of the effects of their blackness in a corporate setting
> * Eliminate racial stereotypes
> * Eliminate whites' concerns about reverse discrimination because career plans are usually worked up and down the hierarchy, with agreement from key people.

The results of Mayor's (1996) British investigation of the career development of 'black' nurses in the NHS, also emphasised the importance of early and strategic career planning strategies by those who attained leadership positions. These women did not leave their career trajectories to chance but had been managed through assessment of personal development needs, developing and nurturing networks for peer support, developing skills both in and outside the job, self-funded study, and gaining the appropriate experience at practitioner level (Mayor, 1996).

Many of the highly successful black and ethnic minority female management interviewees had often tended to reach upper levels of the organisation by resisting the organisational pressures to socialise them into behaving in ways which adapted to the organisational norm. They refused to 'blend in' and become 'invisible', rather they were likely to acquire leadership skills which made them stand out from other colleagues. This was appropriately summarised by Dickens and Dickens (1991):

> What all this means is that to push beyond the invisible barrier into the upper levels of management, people – blacks in particular – must fight against the organisational socialisation they have undergone. To move ahead, the individual manager must distinguish himself or herself from the other middle-level managers; he or she must become a 'leader'.

PREJUDICED ATTITUDES – 'THINK MANAGER – THINK WHITE MALE'

One of the major career barriers facing women managers today is the continued biased attitude towards women based on the sex-role stereotyping of the managerial position. That is, the perception that the characteristics required for success as a manager are more likely to be held by men, in general, than by women in general. In other words, the general perceptions to 'think manager, think male' (Schein, 1994).

Examining attitudes towards women managers and women in general by males is particularly important, taking into account the survey of 1,500 female managers and 800 male managers, carried out by the UK Institute of Management on its members (Institute of Management, 1992). While 74% of women 'strongly agreed' that women managers brought positive skills to the workplace, only one-third of men believed this to be the case. Furthermore, nearly 20% of men maintained they would find it difficult to work for a woman. Their reasons were combined in the remark: 'In general, women do not make good managers – although they have much to offer in the workplace.'

In the USA, Brenner *et al.*, (1989) and Schein *et al.*, (1989) carried out 15 year follow-up studies on the relationship between sex-role stereotypes and requisite management characteristics. These surveys revealed that unlike women in the 1970s, American female managers and female management students today do not sex type the managerial position, but view women and men as equally likely to possess characteristics necessary for managerial success. However, American male management students viewed the management position in the same way as US male managers and male managers in the 1970s. All three male groups believed that, compared with women, men were more likely to possess characteristics necessary for managerial success.

More recently, Schein and Davidson (1993) were interested to discover the managerial sex typing attitudes of future managers and captains of industry in Britain. Their study used 379 British male and female management undergraduate students and examined the extent to which males and females 'think manager – think male', using the Schein Descriptive Index which defines sex role stereotypes and the characteristics of successful managers. The results confirmed that 'think manager – think male' is a strongly held attitude among British undergraduate male management students. These outcomes are similar to those found among US male management students (Schein *et al.*, 1989) and German male business students (Schein and Mueller, 1992). Although the British female undergraduate management sample also sex typed the managerial position, it was to a lesser extent than their male counterparts.

An examination of the specific item rating provided some understanding of how managerial sex typing can impact negatively on women's managerial opportunities. Characteristics such as leadership ability and skilled business matters would be considered as very important to effectiveness by most management theorists and practitioners. Yet, according to Schein and Davidson's (1993) results, women are less likely than men to possess these characteristics. If this view is held by current managers as well, it is no wonder that so many of the male managers surveyed by the Institute of Management (1992) believed that women did not make good managers. All else being equal, the perceived similarity between the characteristics of successful middle managers and men in general increases the likelihood of a male rather than a female being selected for or promoted into, a managerial position. As such, future managers and leaders of Britain's business organisations can be expected to view women as less qualified for managerial positions, and make selection, placement and promotion decisions that impact negatively on women's advancement.

With the American research confirming that black and ethnic minority managers, particularly women, are doubly disadvantaged in terms of upward mobility (Bell, 1990; Greenhaus *et al.*, 1990), the evidence also suggests that they are subjected to the sex and ethnic role stereotyping of the managerial job, i.e. 'think manager – think *white* male'. Hence, they are much more likely to face the barriers of a 'concrete ceiling' related to treatment discrimination. One woman manager interviewee who was a management trainer on a residential training course recalled a 'typical' reaction from a white male manager who eventually revealed his stereotypical assumptions which typified 'think manager – think white male'. He recounted: 'When I first saw you coming down the hotel staircase I immediately assumed you were a model or a receptionist. I was amazed when I first walked into the conference room and discovered you were actually running the course!'

In the past it has been proposed that a major problem for women professionals, hampering their career development, was their fear of promotion and lack of ambition compared to men professionals. However, recent studies have shown no such differences and in the survey of British Institute of Managers' members, women managers viewed themselves as more sociable, intellectual and ambitious than the men (Nicholson and West, 1988). This was also confirmed by the sample of 30 black and ethnic minority women managers. Only one of the women managers viewed herself as less ambitious than either her white male or female colleagues, 40% saw themselves as being equally ambitious and over half (57%) believed they were even more ambitious.

NETWORKING

Dickens and Dickens (1991) propose that infiltrating white and black network systems is an important career progression tool for black and ethnic minority managers at all four phases of career development. In particular, Bell (1990) suggests that previous literature indicates that black and ethnic minority female managers are often omitted from important networks and isolated from people who can help them develop their professional skills and enhance career development. Vinnicombe and Colwill (1995) define networking as the bonding together of like-minded people for the purposes of contact and friendship and support. Certainly evidence supports that women in management generally often find it difficult to break into the male-dominated 'old boy network' and therefore are denied the contacts, opportunities and policy information it provides (Davidson and Cooper, 1992; Wilson, 1995). There are also indications that women managers are more likely than men to use networks for social rather than career support. Vinnicombe and Colwill for example, quote a British study in which twice the percentage of male senior executives (70%) compared to female senior executives, found their jobs through networking (Zoltie and Clarke, 1993). Fitzgerald (1986) refers to research by Becker in the US in the late 1970s which indicated that 'blacks' have less access to personal networks which included whites who could act as job intermediaries or referees. Fitzgerald (1986) concluded: 'Assuming that white employers would put more credence in "white" references, this segregation not only places blacks at a hiring disadvantage, but also cuts them off from the informal networking which is so useful in the job search process.' Dickens and Dickens (1991) emphasise the need for 'black' managers to utilise successfully both white and black networks as support systems throughout all four of the career progression phases.

In response to the so called 'old boy network', the formation of women's network groups has seen a rapid growth over the past decade. These have included professional and occupational networks, in-company networks and training networks (Vinnicombe and Colwill, 1995). More recently, there has been a new surge of networks specifically aimed at black and ethnic minority employees (both male and female), particularly in the public sector (LARRIE, 1995). The Bradford Local Authority, for example, established a Black People into Management Group in 1992 and numerous other local authorities are now introducing positive action and training programmes specifically designed for black and other minority ethnic managers (LARRIE, 1995). Similar initiatives are being introduced in some private sector companies such as British Telecom, who have introduced a black Employees' Network.

White's (1990) research investigating a number of American organisations, discovered that white women and men were more likely to network with each other than with blacks or other ethnic minorities. While white women were more likely to network by setting up informal gatherings such as cocktail parties, African-American women tended to network and socialise through 'black' colleagues or 'black' associations. One such 'black' association, a computer manufacturing firm, counselled, advised and assisted when trouble developed as well as helping blacks move into vacated positions and providing job specific skills. This association was particularly successful at the upper levels of management and was a vehicle where the majority of the African-American women did their formal and informal networking (White, 1990).

The overall impression from the interview sample, was that joining formal, predominantly white, network groups was often viewed as unattractive and sometimes problematic. A third had never joined any formal network group at all and only three had joined a predominantly white male and female network. While just over a third had joined white female network groups, many voiced concern about not feeling they really 'fitted in' either because they felt the members were too radical/feminist or because of their different ethnic background. As one African interviewee recalled:

> I used to belong to a Women in Management Network Group. I paid my membership fee and everything. However, I only ever went to one meeting. I was the only black woman there and I felt uncomfortable. I didn't feel I fitted in. I would really appreciate the chance to join a black women's network but there aren't any for me at the moment.

Certainly, many of the women interviewed said they would benefit from joining a 'black' women in management network. A number maintained they planned to initiate such a network and the vast majority of interviewees asked for contact names and addresses of other women who had participated in the study. Four women had already joined a 'black' female network and seven had joined a 'black' network for males and females.

Many women interviewed said they carried out informal networking, particularly seeking out other 'black' women in similar positions to their own. Denton (1990) highlighted the kind of support 'black' women are provided with by their bonds with other 'black' women. In a two-day assessment workshop, 71 African-American professional women maintained that the highest levels of growth and development from this type of bonding resulted from support functions involving emotional support, high commitment to one another, and encouragement to tackle life's obstacles.

Certainly it was found that a number of the women interviewees did feel that they were excluded from the informal networks practised by their white female managerial colleagues:

> The 'old boy network' (white) in this organisation is very strong and you've little chance of infiltrating it if you're a white woman, never mind a black one. My white female colleagues have quite a strong informal network of their own but I know I'm only partially accepted. I often discover they've had informal gatherings at lunchtime or after work and I haven't been invited. I don't think its always deliberate on their part, I think they just forget to ask me. They don't really see me as one of them I suppose.

Williams (1989) reported that 42% of her African-American female college administrators felt somewhat excluded from the information and support network. She emphasised the importance of informal support networks by concluding: 'The support network and the feeling of being part of the administrative team is important for an individual's success since the feeling of team involvement centres around the concept of trust.'

MENTORING

Mentoring can be either formal, that is, part of the formal organisational policy, or informal, a private arrangement between two individuals, a mentor and a protégé, which does not necessarily have organisational approval. While the majority of mentoring relationships are informal, formal mentoring schemes are increasingly being introduced both in public and private sectors. Generally, a mentor provides information, advice and support for a junior person in a relationship lasting over an extended period of time, marked by substantial emotional commitment from both partners.

Research which was concentrated on successful men and women, indicates that individuals can identify people who have acted as mentors. A study on US male and female employees supported the view that individuals' reported job/career experiences and their protégé status were related. Individuals who were mentored were found to report having more advantages in career/job outcomes than those who were not mentored, regardless of their sex or level (Fagenson, 1989). Cox and Cooper's (1988) British study of male high flyers, found that all the managing directors had had a mentor, usually informal, who was usually an immediate boss.

While there have been many studies investigating the role of mentors in the career development of male managers, there has been very little British research carried out on women managers and mentoring. Clutterbuck and Devine (1987) surveyed 98 randomly selected UK women managers and entrepreneurs and 94% of the sample reported that a mentor had a significantly beneficial effect on their career development. The most commonly mentioned benefits included improved self-confidence and self-image and being made more visible to senior management. A quarter of the sample maintained mentors aided them to focus their aspirations and 18% reported that they acted as role models. Similar results were found by a recent study of 48 successful white British women in which 87% said they had had a mentor, the majority being male, who had been influential in their careers (White, Cox and Cooper, 1992).

Another study of 10 male and 20 female white UK managers involving in-depth interviews, revealed that the majority believed their mentors were important in introducing them to the formal network of power relations which existed in the organisation. Furthermore, a significant finding was that of the five women who had not experienced a mentoring relationship, most reported feeling disadvantaged in terms of gaining access to these informal networks (Arnold and Davidson, 1990). Nevertheless, there appear to be some distinct differences in the mentoring experiences of men and women managers. First, women managers appear to express greater need than men for psychological affirmation from their mentors particularly in relation to building self-confidence (Arnold and Davidson, 1990; White, Cox and Cooper, 1992). Secondly, due to the common absence of women in senior positions, more women than men are likely to be in 'cross-gender' relationships where role modelling is more problematic. Moreover, a disturbing finding revealed by Arnold and Davidson (1990) concerned the high proportion of women managers, predominantly in cross-gender mentoring relationships, who reported problems internal to the relationship. Twenty one per cent of women reported incidences of their male mentor actually blocking their career development. Reasons varied from feeling they were a threat to their male mentor, to believing their male mentor did not want to lose them via promotion. Finally, another problem related to cross-gender relationships for both male and particularly female protégés, was that of gossip, which usually implied sexual liaisons (Arnold and Davidson, 1990).

MENTORS AND PROTÉGÉS – THE IMPACT OF RACE

Dickens and Dickens (1991) assert that seeking sponsors/mentors is an important progression for black and ethnic minority managers in the Planned Growth Phase of Career Development (see Figure 6.1). Nevertheless, these authors acknowledge the difficulties faced and state:

> One very big problem for blacks getting sponsored is that white managers are still often not able to recognise minority potential. Blacks tend to bear little resemblance to how the white organisation thinks its managers should look and behave. Establishing a social relationship is difficult because the pressures

of differing cultures, differing expectations of each other, and personal and institutional prejudices are always there to interfere.

(Dickens and Dickens, 1991)

Bell (1990) supports this argument and suggests that African-American managers, particularly female managers, are more likely than their white counterparts to encounter difficulties finding mentors to provide guidance for moving up the organisational hierarchy. Certainly, there is some evidence in the literature that black and ethnic minority managers are less likely than white managers to report having even had a mentor. In his American study of black and ethnic minority male entrepreneurs, Herbert (1989) declared:

> Among the most significant findings of this investigation, was the absence and apparent insignificance of the formation of mentoring relationships for the black entrepreneurs. No evidence of *any* kind of mentoring was found among these black men. There was no cross-racial mentoring, no cross-gender mentoring, and no black-on-black mentoring.

However, Thomas (1989) tends to refute this claim and points out that studies by Herbert (1989) and Gooden (1981), which reported that the majority of 'blacks' did not have a mentor, used small sample sizes. Larger survey studies by Ford and Wells (1985) of 80 'black' public administrators and executives and Murray's (1982) study of middle class 'black' men, both found that 51% had mentors. Thomas (1989) makes the important observation that one needs to take into account the availability of potential black and ethnic minority mentors within organisational settings, which often determines the frequency of such relationships as well as the racial dynamics. The 'black' respondents in the Ford and Wells (1985) study worked in a mixed racial environment and the majority had 'black' mentors, while the majority of 'black' respondents in the study by Murray (1982), working in predominantly white corporations, reported having white mentors. This may also explain why a high 82% of 'black' female public administrators, in mixed race work environments, reported having predominantly 'black' mentors (Malone, 1981) compared to only 37% of black female administrators working in predominantly white American colleges, where most of the mentors were white (Williams, 1989).

When the sample of black and ethnic minority women managers were asked whether they had *ever had* a mentor, rather than whether they currently had a mentor, only 43% reported experiencing a mentoring relationship. This is in sharp contrast with the previous studies of British white female managers in which between 87% (White, Cox and Cooper, 1982) and 94% (Clutterbuck and Devine, 1987) reported having had at least one mentor. Of the 16 women interviewees who had had a mentor, 7 instances were with a white male mentor, 5 with a white female mentor, and only 4 instances with black female mentors.

According to Thomas (1989):

Cross-race/cross-gender relationships pose special difficulties by activating a triangle of relationships. A black man mentoring a white female may upset white men. A black female's supportive alliance with a white man can upset a black man. Same-sex/cross-race relationships pose different and somewhat less volatile dynamics.

In his article on 'black' experiences of mentoring, Thomas (1989) views sex and race taboos, combined also with the black American's history of slavery, as critically shaping the dynamics of cross-race relationships, as illustrated in Table 6.1.

For Thomas (1989), racial difference and sex and race taboos can significantly hamper feelings of closeness and identification between 'blacks' and whites. He also suggests that identification with the protégé by the mentor, reduces the uncertainty and risk in terms of the protégé's performance. However, he comments:

> the care anxiety of mentoring – the dread of what can't be predicted – is filled out by the culture of racism. It is this set of feelings, which obscures the white manager's vision of the goodness in blacks. Hence, these triangle of taboos significantly blocks cross-sex/cross-race mentoring relationships.

Many of the women manager interviewees, who hadn't had mentors, said it had been difficult finding anyone, particularly a 'black' female, who could also act as a role model. One lamented: 'I would have loved to have had a mentor. It's been a problem for me as I've never been able to find someone. In particular I would have liked a black female mentor.'

Thomas's (1989) American study of 88 'black' and 107 white managers and mentoring relationships, found that 'black' protégés formed 63% of their mentoring relationships with whites but same-race relationships provided significantly more psychosocial support than cross-race relationships. This is of particular relevance for black and ethnic minority women managers, taking into account previous studies on white managers, which suggests the importance of psychosocial support for female white protégés

Table 6.1   Relationships (ranked by power to evoke taboos)

Rank order	Relationship	Tabooed feeling
1	White male superior Black female subordinate	White man having unlimited sexual access to black woman
1	Black male superior White female subordinate	Black man sexually approaching a white woman
2	White male superior Black male subordinate	White man 'freeing a slave', threatening other white men
2	White female superior Black female subordinate	Black woman abandoning her men, counter-balanced by shared experience of womanhood

Source: Adapted from Thomas, 1989, p. 285.

(Arnold and Davidson. 1990; White, Cox and Cooper, 1992). Thomas (1989) also reported that 'blacks' were more likely than whites to form relationships outside their departments and the formal lines of authority. This certainly appeared to be the trend for the women interviewees who had 'black' mentors, all of whom had been women. In addition, as previously discussed in Chapter 2, black role models from childhood, e.g. mothers, teachers, had often acted as important influences. One woman said: 'My only mentor has been the supervisor of my masters degree who is a black woman. I meet her for a few hours every month and she has taken over as a mentor for me both in my studies and in work related matters.' Another interviewee had found a valuable 'black' female mentor, who was based in the USA. Another had met an African-American woman through her work from whom she got tremendous personal support in the mentoring relationship and met up with regularly at weekends at her home to discuss work issues over coffee.

It should be emphasised that those women in the study who reported having had a white mentor, either male or female, viewed the experience as a positive one. This is typified by the following quote from an Afro-Caribbean woman who now holds a very senior executive position:

> My previous mentor was a Principal Nursing Officer who was a white male. When I was turned down for yet another job the second time, I was so angry, I wanted to leave. He told me not to. He told me 'don't let them beat you – use this experience in a positive way, let it energise you.' So I did. They said that I didn't get the job because I lacked budgeting knowledge, so with his support, I made them send me on a course even though it cost them £75 a day.

All in all, the material gathered from the interviews indicated that black and ethnic minority women managers appear to be less likely than their female white counterparts to have experienced a mentoring relationship and the majority maintained they would have benefited from having had a 'black' female mentor. These findings lend strong support to Thomas's (1989) recommendation when he stated:

> Organisations would do well to support blacks in their efforts to build supportive developmental relationships with other blacks in the workplace. If same-race relationships are major sources of psychosocial support, blacks who do not have access to such relationships may have very unbalanced work lives or social development, which will result in problems later in their careers.

In Britain, particularly in the public and education sectors, a limited number of 'black' and ethnic minority mentoring schemes have recently been introduced. The Leeds Mentor Project for example, was established in 1993 and aims to offer help and guidance to adult trainees from educationally disadvantaged groups, mainly ethnic minorities, refugees and migrants, women returners and people with special needs (Yaghmaiepour-Urwin and Zulfiquar, 1994). The BBC Mentor Project for students was implemented in

BBC Network Television and News and Current Affairs Directorates in 1994 (Holder, 1995). Manchester City College offers a mentoring service aimed at improving the career prospects of ethnic minority students by pairing them with relevant professional role models from their own communities (City College, Manchester, 1995). Another university, Goldsmiths, University of London has started a Black Teachers Mentoring scheme in order to create a support network of members/protégés to help redress the under-representation of black and ethnic minority teachers in the profession, including 'black' students entering Higher Education, and to improve the retention rates of black and ethnic minority teachers (Popeau, 1995). Finally, an example of a mentoring scheme aimed specifically at ethnic minority managers (in this case black Afro-Caribbean men) has been introduced by Imani Venture in Birmingham (Treasure-Garwood, 1993). This programme aimed to match Afro-Caribbean male students with professional mentors, offering them appropriate work placements, teaching them management and related skills, and helping them to form strategies for gaining professional employment.

Formal mentoring schemes of any kind have been shown to be potentially problematic, particularly if the assigned mentor and/or protégé is unhappy with his/her role and pairing, and is untrained (Davidson and Cooper, 1992). However, all the aforementioned ethnic minority mentoring schemes included training and briefings of varying degrees for both mentors and protégés. There is an obvious need for future research to fully evaluate the benefits and good practice strategies of such mentoring schemes to encourage their adoption by more and more organisations, particularly in the private sector. Mentor Training Services (1995) have, for example, been one such pioneer by developing a comprehensive Mentor Pack based on the experiences of five successful Mentoring Schemes providing support to 387 students, including ethnic minorities, attending City and Islington College in London. According to Mentor Training Services (1995): 'The experience of the North London Programme clearly demonstrates that a Mentoring approach can really enhance the personal development and career prospects of a range of people.'

CONCLUSIONS

There is an urgent need for organisations to break down some of the specific career barriers facing black and ethnic minority women managers outlined in this chapter. Adopting Dickens and Dickens (1991) career phase model for black and ethnic minority managers presented in Figure 6.1, the female management interviewees in the sample who were in the Entry and Adjustment Phases, were most at risk in terms of suffering hardships due to racism and sexism. Furthermore, compared to their white female managerial counterparts, these women appear to be more likely to:

- receive lower pay;
- face racial and sexual discrimination in relation to getting jobs and promotion;
- be subject to racial job ghettoisation;
- encounter ethnic role stereotyping of the managerial job, i.e. 'think manager – think *white* male'.

In addition, companies and professional bodies should create black and ethnic minority women in management network groups and mentoring schemes in order to combat the isolation of these women. As well, they should also provide early social and career advice/support mechanisms which these women would undoubtedly benefit from, starting at the Entry Phase. LARRIE (Local Authorities Race Relations Information Exchange) publishes reports based on information from their database, on local authority initiatives for the support and development of black and minority ethic managers. However, compared to the efforts that the majority of local authorities with active equal opportunities in employment policies are making to ensure that equal opportunities are being achieved in recruitment and selection, evidence suggests they are failing to adopt the same effort in other areas such as staff development and training (LARRIE, 1995; CRE, 1995; African and Caribbean Finance Forum *et al.*, 1996). A recent report by the African and Caribbean Finance Forum *et al.* entitled *The Cement Roof – Afro-Caribbean People in Management* stated:

> Interviews with Afro-Caribbean employees acknowledge that the overall situation has improved since their parents/grandparents first arrived in the UK, but there is still a long way to go before the cement roof is broken through. . . . There is little knowledge amongst employers of the barriers to equality; many are complacent and few, if any, have the issue high on their list of priorities.

7

Positive Approaches to Helping Black and Ethnic Minority Women into Management

Rather than Equal Opportunity Policies, what is needed is Positive Action. There have been quota systems for white male managers for centuries, but no-one calls that discrimination!

Throughout this book, the main difficulties faced by black and ethnic minority women managers at work and at home have been outlined. The model in Figure 7.1 summarises a typical profile, and major problems/pressures at work, home and socially and negative outcomes in terms of career progression and stress of the black and ethnic minority woman manager compared to her white female counterpart. Demographically, black and ethnic minority women in management appear to be more likely to be first borns, tend to be more highly educated and are much more likely to be married with children. Indications are that they will have a greater chance of earning more than their partner, are more likely than white female managers to be in a mixed racial partnership and if Afro-Caribbean, have a greater tendency to be a single parent. In the work arena, they are faced with prejudice and discrimination stemming from the double bind of racism and sexism, combined with the problems associated with the domination of white, male organisational cultural norms and values. These stresses and strains linked to token 'black' woman issues, relationship problems and blocked career opportunities all contribute towards their difficulties in 'cracking the concrete ceiling'.

At work, home and socially, unlike white women managers, they are often faced with bicultural identity/status role stress – constant switching between white and 'black' cultures; traditions, norms and values. The costs in terms of negative outcomes and stress include job dissatisfaction, impaired job performance, physical and psychological ill health, tiredness and loss of confidence. One of the most disturbing findings from this study, was the overriding fact that the majority of these women managers were so disillusioned with the 'concrete ceiling' that *over 80% planned to leave their present company in the near future.* Seventy per cent aimed to get a better

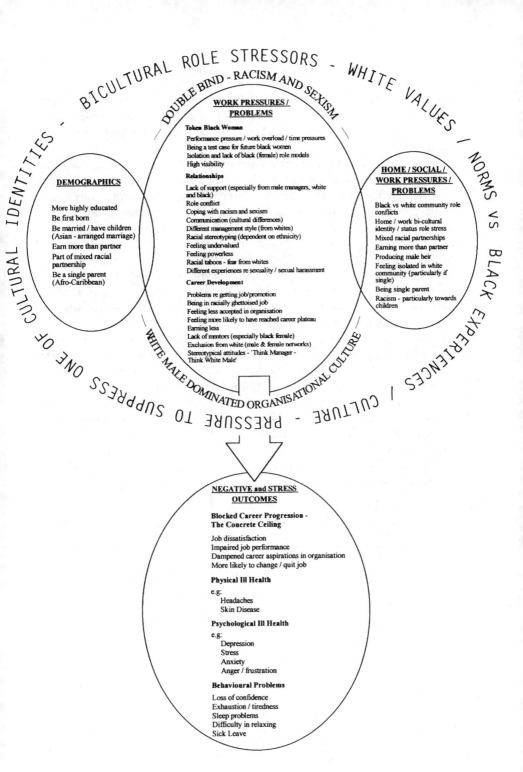

BICULTURAL ROLE STRESSORS - WHITE VALUES / NORMS VS BLACK EXPERIENCES / CULTURE - PRESSURE TO SUPPRESS ONE OF CULTURAL IDENTITIES - DOUBLE BIND - RACISM AND SEXISM

WHITE MALE DOMINATED ORGANISATIONAL CULTURE

DEMOGRAPHICS

More highly educated
Be first born
Be married / have children (Asian - arranged marriage)
Earn more than partner
Part of mixed racial partnership
Be a single parent (Afro-Caribbean)

WORK PRESSURES / PROBLEMS

Token Black Woman

Performance pressure / work overload / time pressures
Being a test case for future black women
Isolation and lack of black (female) role models
High visibility

Relationships

Lack of support (especially from male managers, white and black)
Role conflict
Coping with racism and sexism
Communication (cultural differences)
Different management style (from whites)
Racial stereotyping (dependent on ethnicity)
Feeling undervalued
Feeling powerless
Racial taboos - fear from whites
Different experiences re sexuality / sexual harassment

Career Development

Problems re getting job/promotion
Being in racially ghettoised job
Feeling less accepted in organisation
Feeling more likely to have reached career plateau
Earning less
Lack of mentors (especially black female)
Exclusion from white (male & female networks)
Stereotypical attitudes - 'Think Manager - Think White Male'

HOME / SOCIAL / WORK PRESSURES / PROBLEMS

Black vs white community role conflicts
Home / work bi-cultural identity / status role stress
Mixed racial partnerships
Earning more than partner
Producing male heir
Feeling isolated in white community (particularly if single)
Being single parent
Racism - particularly towards children

NEGATIVE and STRESS OUTCOMES

Blocked Career Progression - The Concrete Ceiling

Job dissatisfaction
Impaired job performance
Dampened career aspirations in organisation
More likely to change / quit job

Physical Ill Health

e.g:
    Headaches
    Skin Disease

Psychological Ill Health

e.g:
    Depression
    Stress
    Anxiety
    Anger / frustration

Behavioural Problems

Loss of confidence
Exhaustion / tiredness
Sleep problems
Difficulty in relaxing
Sick Leave

Figure 7.1 The black and ethnic minority woman manager – a model to illustrate the typical profile, pressures/problems and negative outcomes/stress compared to her white female counterpart

job with other 'more enlightened' organisations and 10% were planning to leave and set up their own business. Out of a total of 30 women interviewed, only one saw herself as gaining a higher position within the same company

While the preceding chapters have outlined some strategies which black and ethnic minority women themselves may adopt in order to manipulate, control and juggle these bicultural largely 'white-man-made' barriers, a number of organisational initiatives (e.g. 'black' mentoring schemes etc.) have also been described. In the past, the author has consistently asserted that the position of white women managers will only improve by any substantial degree through attitudinal, legal and organisational changes and initiatives (Davidson and Cooper, 1992; Davidson, 1996). The arguments for such initiatives aimed at tackling both racial and sexual discriminatory barriers, are *twice as strong* if organisations and governments wish to ensure equality of opportunity for black and ethnic minority women wishing to enter management. Briscoe and Wilson's (1992) forecasts in economic activity rates up to the year 2000, predict that women are likely to increase their share in almost all occupations, particularly in the managerial, professional and associated professional areas where they are currently under-represented. Table 7.1 illustrates that in the IER's forecasts of occupational change 1991–2000, ethnic minority women are disproportionately concentrated in declining industries, and under-represented in the expanding sectors. Bhavnani (1994) makes the important point that with the growth of Compulsory Competitive Tendering (CCT), the abolition of Wages Councils and the restructuring of finance and other white collar

Table 7.1 Occupational change 1991–2000: the pattern of women's employment by ethnic group in 1989

Sub-major groups forecast to expand female employment by over 35%, 1991–2000	Percentage of each ethnic group employed in the designated occupations in 1989		
	White women	Black women	Other
1.1 Corporate managers	4.9	1.7	7.0
2.1 Science and engineering professionals	0.5	0.4	0.6
2.2 Health professionals	10.4	2.2	0.0
2.4 Other professional occupations	0.8	0.6	0.0
3.1 Science- and engineering-associated professions	0.0	0.0	0.0
3.3 Other associated professional occupations	0.8	0.3	4.2
TOTAL	**17.4**	**5.2**	**11.8**
Sub-major groups forecast to contract female employment by over 40%, 1991–2000			
5.3 Other skilled trades	4.2	13.6	4.5
8.1 Industrial plant and machine operators	7.1	16.8	4.7
TOTAL	**11.3**	**30.4**	**9.1**

Source: Equal Opportunities Review (1994), No. 56, July/August, p. 22

work, the indications are that generally, the increase of black women's employment levels will be 'a deteriorating situation'.

The proportion of ethnic minority women in the labour force is expected to rise, including increasing numbers of those with qualifications, and corporate managers are one of the sub-major groups forecast to expand female employment by over 35% between 1991 and 2000. Consequently, according to these figures, with 1.7% of corporate managers being black and ethnic minority women in 1989 compared to 4.9% of white women, the percentage of black and ethnic minority women in management should increase by the millennium.

Similar projections have been forecast in the USA and Dickens and Dickens (1991) have stressed the urgency for organisations to address these changes and tackle racism:

> By the year 2000, the majority of new people entering the workforce will be minorities and women, which means that whites will be managing more blacks, women and other minorities. To ensure maximum productivity, efficiency, and teamwork on the part of all their employees, white managers must recognise the occurrence of certain prejudicial acts that interfere with the job performance of blacks, accept their own responsibility for training blacks to manage racist behaviour and learn how to manage the racist behaviour of other whites.

Hence, this chapter will focus on individual strategies for success as well as what organisations, employers, governments and unions can do to make life easier for black and ethnic minority women managers, and emphasise the need for changing attitudes and behaviour.

STRATEGIES FOR SUCCESS

American literature pertaining to explain the dearth of black and ethnic minority women in management, particularly in senior positions has proposed numerous reasons and intervening variables. These include the pipeline theory, i.e. black and ethnic minority women have not been in their corporate positions long enough and in sufficient numbers to gain the attention and confidence of senior management; rate of growth of a particular company, and whether or not the business is 'black owned' (Fulbright, 1986). However, White (1990) criticises the pipeline theory and its emphasis on length of service for failing to take into consideration important factors such as racism and discrimination. Indeed, White's (1990) analysis of in-depth interviews with US African-American senior female managers and the subsequent conclusions, very much supports findings presented throughout this book. According to White (1990): 'Discrimination is a significant barrier to black women seeking to enter corporations in general, much less senior management.' She hypothesised that the two main determinants for these women's success in the corporate culture which can counteract the deliberating effects of institutional discrimination and racism centre on:

1. strategies;
2. skills.

Based on White's (1990) interview data, the following main determinants affected the success of black and ethnic minority women in their interaction with the corporate culture:

1. Strategies
   - Risk taking
   - Campaigning
   - Networking/mentoring
2. Skills
   - Technical/management skills
   - Social skills

Interestingly, these determinants for success certainly appeared to also be substantiated by many of the 30 black and ethnic minority female managerial interviewees. In addition to their own personal experiences, these strategies and skills were also illustrated by the answers they gave when asked what advice they would give to other ethnic minority women starting a management career.

Risk Taking

White (1990) viewed risk taking as a vehicle for enhancing visibility through the attention of upper management, by success in potentially high risk career or job/task assignments. One successful senior manager we interviewed also emphasised the importance of self-promotion in these situations. 'Remember to always take credit for what you have done. Shout about your successes to those in senior management who need to know. I can assure you, if you don't, no one else will!' As part of this process, a large number of participants in the study emphasised the enormous importance of maintaining high self-esteem, confidence in abilities and sheer guts and perseverance, as illustrated by the following quotations:

> You always need to keep your eyes fixed on a goal, believe you can do it and that nobody is better than you are.

> Be true to yourself, know yourself, don't compromise and never give up.

> You have to be confident in your abilities, have the drive to achieve your goals, and never become disillusioned – you must persevere.

> Believing in yourself is really important. If you believe the negative stereotypes, then it will become a self fulfilling prophecy. You have to think and be positive.

Campaigning

Campaigning is all about letting your career aspirations be known to superiors and their colleagues and associates. White (1990) proposes that this can involve a certain amount of risk, particularly if the woman manager lacks credibility. Nevertheless, White reported that almost all her African-American senior female managers believed that many black women were naive in their belief that if they did their present job well, then they would be bound eventually, to get promoted. According to White (1990): 'Black women should ultimately realise that no one is going to hand them a position in senior management on a silver platter. They must instead do battle in the form of an effectively waged campaign.' Two successful senior executive interviewees in the sample also highlighted the importance of this campaigning strategy and one advocated, wrongly or rightly, not taking her ethnicity into the workplace:

> You have to be very positive, very professional. You need to ensure that you plan your career, are seen to plan your career and let your boss know your ambitions. You should leave your ethnicity at home.

> You must be persistent and not give up. Do your homework well and ensure that you contact people who make the decisions and let them know about you and your career aspirations. Women tend to always go for jobs they *know* they can get – men are much more likely to take risks.

Networking and Mentoring

The importance of networking and acquiring mentors as a career strategy has already been discussed in Chapter 6. Many of the women in the sample felt that they had to infiltrate both 'black' (if possible) and white networks, acquire mentors and at the same time, ensure they kept their own identity:

> You need to try and access black women's networks but also management networks within the organisation. Even though these are predominantly white, you have to take and get what you can from them.

> Get a lot of relevant training and find mentors. These should be people who are sympathetic towards you and do not have the power to fire you. You need support to challenge organisations. Go for it. You need good support networks but always remember to keep your own identity.

Management and Social Skills

Appropriate management leadership skills along with the social skills so crucial in implementing the networking/mentoring and campaigning strategies have already been outlined in more depth (see Chapter 6). Integral to this whole process, the women interviewed very much emphasised the enormous relevance of believing in yourself, valuing yourself and *not* allowing the potential burdens of being a 'black' woman manager, to get you down:

> You have to face reality and the fact that you need to arm yourself in terms of excellent training and education – you'll need to be better than your white counterpart. Sad, but true. You also need to be clear about your role – be persistent but also be diplomatic – otherwise you'll be seen as having a chip on your shoulder.

> You've got to learn the interpersonal skills first – when you get an opportunity – *grab it*! Just keep going for it – if you have an unsupportive boss – don't hang around – find another job. Never be daunted by anything – keep trying.

> Get to know 'who is who' in the organisation. Isolate the good people (black and white) and build up good working relationships with them. Believe in yourself and value yourself – don't give in. If things go wrong, being a black person, its more of a double burden but don't let it get you down. Start valuing black people – the fact that they actually contribute to the organisation and the skills, experiences and contacts they bring.

Facing Reality

These strategies and skills outlined by White (1990) and peppered throughout this book, are all ways of counteracting the harsh effects of racial and sexual discrimination – beyond the concrete ceiling. Nevertheless, the interviewees often went to great lengths to emphasise the current reality of the situation for future black and ethnic minority women who wished to pursue a career in management:

> I would advise any other black woman to go for it, but you are going to have to be thick skinned – it isn't going to be a easy ride.

> You will undoubtedly endure some hardships in order to achieve what you want. You need to be one step ahead and will have to be better than your white counterparts.

> I would advise anyone to look into it very carefully before they go into it. The rewards are there, but there is pain and suffering to the individual.

Continuing the theme of 'Facing Reality' and the situation encountered by black and ethnic minority managers in the workplace, Dickens and Dickens (1991) have detailed and summarised the following main strategies. These encapsulate the strategies previously outlined throughout this book which can be adopted by black and ethnic minority women managers.

- Joining up quickly to an organisation and producing results immediately.
- Planning for success, i.e. career planning early.
- Finding mentors and sponsors and being seen and evaluated by senior management.
- Resisting oversocialisation and not discounting those unique qualities which one's ethnicity brings to the organisation.

- Developing productive work relationships.
- Understanding the impact of your heritage and being aware of the impact of your 'blackness' in the workplace.
- Learning to manage the racist behaviour of others.

Perhaps one of the most poignant pieces of advice came from a senior executive Afro-Caribbean women interviewee when she said: 'Don't forget your roots, where you came from, or you will lose yourself – the ghost of women in your dreams.'

However, rather than arming black women with strategies to try and move beyond these enormous discriminatory barriers, what is obviously needed is a breakdown of organisational and societal attitudes.

WHAT ORGANISATIONS CAN DO – THE MANAGEMENT OF DIVERSITY

With an increasing number of black women entering management and creating businesses within and outside the traditional corporate structure, it is incumbent on organisations to develop corporate personnel policies that will minimise the current pressures on women from ethnic minorities. The barriers that prevent *all* women (regardless of ethnic origin) from progressing up the organisational hierarchy and the strategies adopted by employers in order to try and create more equal opportunities for women are well documented (see Davidson and Cooper, 1992). Such policies are listed in Table 7.2 and cover selection and promotion procedures, flexible working, mobility issues, age limits, traditional roles and attitudinal barriers.

More and more organisations are not content to wait for legislative changes, but are dragging their male managers into the twenty-first century by ensuring that their hiring and promotion policies force immediate action to include women. For example, over 300 organisations, representing more than a quarter of the UK workforce, have committed themselves to *Opportunity 2000*, a Business in the Community initiative designed to improve the balance of women and men in the workforce. The goals set by the companies by the year 2000 encompass a range of practical steps depending on the particular circumstances and needs of each business. They include: building equal opportunity objectives into management appraisal processes; increasing the representation of women in key areas, including setting targets; increasing maternity retention rates; introducing family-friendly policies; attitude surveys amongst staff; board-level, senior and line management training programmes; and regular reporting of progress in annual reports.

According to their most recent annual report (Opportunity 2000, 1996), compared with 8% in 1994, women now account for 11% of directors in

Table 7.2 Strategies for change

Barriers	Strategies
Organisational barriers	
Unfair selection or promotion procedures	equal opportunities policy
	equal opportunities training
	dual interviewing
	precise job specifications
	objective assessment criteria
	external advertising
	equal opportunity audits
	monitoring
	targets
Inflexible working	senior level part-time/job sharing arrangements
	flexi-time
	working at home
	annual hours
	other flexible arrangements
Mobility	requirement dropped or modified
	dual-career job search
Age limits	requirement dropped
Traditional roles	
Work and family life	career break schemes
	workplace nurseries
	childcare vouchers
	parental leave
	enhanced maternity leave
	other childcare help
Attitudinal barriers	
Lack of confidence	equal opportunity advertising
	headhunting
	internal promotion policies
	women-only training courses
Prejudice	boardroom commitment to change
	equal opportunities training for managers
	awareness training for all staff

Source: Hansard Society Commission (1990)

member organisations. The percentage of women in senior management rose from 12% in 1994 to 17% in 1996, and in middle management from 24% to 31%. Moreover by 1996, 41% of junior managers were female, a rise of 2% since 1994. Compared to 25% in 1994, overall women accounted for almost one third (31.2%) of all managers. These findings contrast sharply with the latest National Management Salary Survey published by the Institute of Management and Remuneration Economics (1996) which revealed that only 12.3% of managers in the UK are women and 3.3% are directors (see Chapter 1). The campaign therefore suggests that: 'Opportunity 2000 members are likely to employ more females in management than others outside the campaign' (Opportunity 2000, 1996).

Nevertheless, Opportunity 2000 has been previously criticised for ignoring the plight of ethnic minority female managers. As a consequence, for the first time in 1995, campaign members were requested to provide ethnic minority data which illustrated the poor representation of this group of women at management level even in Opportunity 2000 organisational membership. For example, at middle management level, 'black' women accounted for only 1% and Asian women for only 0.9% (Opportunity 2000, 1995). Clearly, *specific* policies and practices need to be focused and made applicable to ethnic minority women. *What is evident from all the cumulative evidence presented through this book, is that racial, as well as gender issues need to be targeted specifically in positive action and equal opportunities programmes by organisations. To date, this has obviously tended not to have been the case.*

Organisations which have initiated systematic and structured equal opportunity policies usually carry out equal opportunity audits and monitoring (Sutherland and Davidson, 1996). According to the Hansard Society Commission (1990):

> Equal opportunity audits are designed to provide an organisation with a comprehensive picture of the patterns of employment of women; the effect of the organisation's working arrangements upon the potential for career development among women; the relationship between current recruitment, training, promotion and general employment policies and practices, and the development of equal opportunities; and the attitudes of employers and their supervisors/managers towards the present position and any potential changes.

Audits such as these tend to include both in-depth statistical analysis and in-depth interviews with a cross-section of both males and females throughout the organisation. Based on the results of equal opportunity audits, recommendations for a continued programme of action to overcome actual and potential barriers can be proposed, and periodic monitoring of progress can commence. However, to date, many of these audits have failed to specifically address racial issues, in addition to the gender ones. All too often, ethnic minority factors have only been monitored as part of the demographic data. A large-scale survey of British employers in 1994, for example, found that although 19% had identified as a priority for the future 'actions relating to women', this figure fell to 9% in respect of actions relating to ethnic minorities (African and Caribbean Finance Forum *et al.*, 1996). This was reaffirmed by the Commission for Racial Equality's (CRE, 1995) Standard for Employers publication – *Racial Equality Means Business* which sets out detailed action plans for employers, including those covering staff development:

> An organisation which sets out to value and use the potential of all its workforce needs to identify the factors which may work against this aim for

particular groups. For example, taking action to ensure equal opportunity for women or people with disabilities will not automatically ensure equal treatment for *ethnic minority* women or *ethnic minority* people with disabilities.

A number of national initiatives have been developed, in the field of equal opportunities such as the Department of Employment's *Ten Point Plan*, the Equal Opportunities Commission's Checklist and the *Code of Practice for People with Disabilities*.

The CRE standard can be used in conjunction with these and other, similar initiatives, whether they are implemented as separate programmes or as part of a wider equality strategy.

(CRE, 1995)

This important document can be used as both a planning and measurement tool and the standard covers areas where organisations can apply and use a race quality programme: policy and planning; selection; developing and retaining staff; communication and corporate image; corporate citizenship; and auditing for racial equality. Figure 7.2 details the strategies required at five different levels when an organisation carries out a racial equality audit (CRE, 1995).

In addition to initiatives such as flexible working, family friendly cultures, job share/part-time jobs applicable to all women (see Table 7.2), all the interview sample of black and ethnic minority women managers felt there were numerous Equal Opportunity strategies/policies which should be introduced by organisations. What was interesting, was that the majority of suggestions proposed by these ethnic minority female managers were specifically directed towards breaking down racial discriminatory barriers and prejudices, rather than gender related issues. There was strong support for the implementation of Positive Action Programmes, including Equal Opportunity Audits which specially addressed the racial issues so commonly omitted. Moreover, there was a general consensus felt by the interviewees, that to date, many organisations had failed abysmally to seriously confront these issues:

> There is an enormous amount of skill and talent in black workers but organisations are failing to recognise this fact and are losing out. When organisations do attempt to help ethnic minorities, they often do it badly. They expect people to fit into existing moulds. This, of course, leads to personal strife.

The following list of strategies and accompanying quotations were proposed by one or more of the thirty interviewees and closely mirror many of the action plans outlined by CRE (1995) and mentioned throughout this book:

Specifically investigate the needs of 'black' workers – including Equal Opportunity Audits

> Organisations should stop paying lip service to Equal Opportunities and do something. They need to investigate sexism and racism and tackle it. In particular, they should look at the needs of black women.

Level 1	• Plans have been made to collect ethnic origin data, following consultation with employee representatives, including ethnic minority staff.
	• The areas to be audited have been identified, and the scope of each audit, and type of analysis determined.
	• Publicity has been given to the monitoring programme, and the reasons for it explained.
Level 2	• Information has been collected about sex and ethnic origins of:
	– staff in post;
	– applicants for jobs, promotion, and training;
	– customers and clients using market profiles.
	• Analysis by ethnic origin and sex has been done on data concerning:
	– staff in post (by level, function, section, location, etc.);
	– incidents and complaints of harassment.
	• The data on clients and customers have been analysed to find out how much they benefit from the goods and services provided.
Level 3	• Analysis has been done of the data on applicants and success rates for jobs, promotion, redundancies and training:
	– grievances;
	– disciplinary action;
	– performance appraisal;
	– training;
	– staff dismissed or leaving for other reasons.
	• Progress is being regularly assessed, and annual reports have been submitted to the most senior levels on the following:
	– participation ratios, seniority ratios;
	– application ratios;
	– career progression rates.
	• Revisions have been made to the racial equality programme to deal with barriers in areas such as:
	– selection and assessment criteria;
	– the range of products or services.
	• New targets have been set for short-, medium- and long-term goals, and overall objectives revised.
Level 4	• Employee surveys are being conducted at regular intervals, and after the introduction of new systems and programmes.
	• Profiles of service users and clients have been checked to assess the impact of the racial equality programme.
	• The organisation's programme has been assessed in the light of external developments.
Level 5	• The action taken by the organisation as a corporate citizen is being regularly evaluated.
	• The monitoring results are being published in the annual report, or as a separate document.
	• Improved staff attitudes towards the organisation have been reflected in surveys.

Source: CRE, 1995 reproduced here with permission

Figure 7.2 Auditing for racial equality

Implement a Racial and Equal Opportunities Policy that works

Organisations should strive to have racial equal opportunity policies that work. I will not apply to an organisation unless I feel they are at least attempting to reach this goal – after my last experience of racism at work.

Create a 'black' friendly culture

The culture of many organisations needs to change the way in which it operates and also the cultural messages they give out and how they publicise themselves.

Encourage 'blacks' to apply for jobs by:
* addressing recruitment policies;
* setting targets;
* monitoring;
* breaking down job ghettoisation.

Organisations need to take positive steps to encourage and actively recruit more black women in leadership positions. They need to make it more friendly and black-women oriented. Open up jobs and opportunities and let black people know – 'yes, there is a career here for you'.

Career development for 'black' workers:
* special training and education for black workers;
* black role models in senior positions;
* black mentoring schemes;
* shadowing schemes;
* job secondments;
* introduce black networks.

Organisations need to train and prepare black people for key leadership roles, particularly black women. I would also like to see black mentoring schemes introduced as well as black support networks.

Organisations have to look at career development issues for their black workers and provide opportunities for further education and training. They have to learn to be open to different ways of doing things and respect diversity of experience. Opportunities for secondments for example, would give out strong messages to black people saying – 'yes, you can achieve if you have the talent regardless of your sex or skin colour'.

Special training for blacks should be introduced to make them aware of skills and techniques they must attain. Mentoring and shadowing schemes for example, would help create positive expectations and workable and active procedures and guidelines would help overcome individuals' personal prejudices.

I believe we have to have black role models in senior positions, particularly in the Private Sector. This will help to promote black people both internally and externally. Companies must employ a representative percentage of black ethnic minority men and women at all levels of the hierarchy.

Changing Attitudes of Workers – Race Relations Training and Education

There needs to be education and awareness training related to racial and cultural issues for both black and white workers. Many of the issues we have talked about during this interview need to be freely aired with both whites and blacks. Too many taboos abound. All employees should attend race awareness and equal opportunity courses. Black people shouldn't have to isolate themselves or struggle against all the odds, to survive in a white male environment. We are a diverse, multiracial society and organisations must embrace that diversity within their own culture and value and nurture individuality.

The CRE document very much supports the equal opportunity policies whose strategies are based on the recognition of diversity, both in the workforce and in society (CRE, 1995). Appendix 1 provides a summary of CRE's (1995) checklist of action involved in considering, planning and implementing a racial equality programme. The effective management of diversity in organisations is a clearly defined approach which presents a business case for moving towards a diverse workforce where the skills of *all* groups are recognised (Kandola and Fullerton, 1994). According to CRE (1995): 'Employers are now increasingly aware that, alongside the legal and moral reasons for racial equality, there is a strong business case for taking action to achieve this end.' Based on the diversity approach, this document (CRE, 1995) details the business case for organisations to acknowledge the relationship between fair employment practices and running a business well, by listing the following major advantages:

- using people's talents to the full;
- ensuring that selection decisions and policies are based on objective criteria, and not on unlawful discrimination, prejudice or unfair assumption;
- becoming an employer of choice;
- getting closer to customers and understanding their needs;
- operating internationally with success;
- sustaining a healthy society;
- making the company more attractive to investors;
- making the company more attractive to customers and clients;
- avoiding the costs of discrimination, i.e.
  - litigation;
  - adverse publicity;
  - damage to staff development;
  - higher absenteeism;
  - greater staff turnover.

Many of these advantages were echoed by the black and ethnic female managers when asked what they thought were the advantages of encouraging more 'black' people, particularly women, to enter the field of management:

It makes business sense for organisations that they need to utilise the talents of their workforce to the full and there are many highly talented ethnic minority workers who are at the moment, certainly underutilised.

Organisations should recognise that in order to relate to their customers, they should have black and Asian employees.

Organisations who have black customers should have black employees. For example, I flew to Jamaica recently, and there was *not one* stewardess/ steward on the flight who was black. Yet, a large proportion of the passengers certainly were.

More black women entering management will introduce different manage-ment styles. We will be able to deliver better services particularly to the high proportion of ethnic minority people in Birmingham where I work.

A high proportion of the interviewees also emphasised their belief that increasing the number of black and ethnic minority women managers would help change attitudes, from both 'blacks' and whites, and break down racial stereotypes:

It has got to become the norm, rather than 'this black women is special'. When we are not seen as someone special – stereotyping will stop and black women will no longer have to specialise and be ghettoised, in order to progress. There would also be far more female management role models.

Equal representation is important to change attitudes. More black women managers would enable the black voice to be heard and to speak out.

It will change the way people will think about management. Also, the black community will see women can actually do something besides running a home. Organisations will undoubtedly benefit.

Cassell (1996) points out that the exponents of the management of diversity argue that all differences must be valued including those of white males. Evidence of the benefits of successful management of diversity is particularly strong from the USA and includes being able to recruit from a greater range of talent, being able to retain that talent, and benefiting from the subsequent savings from lower absenteeism and turnover (Kandola and Fullerton, 1994). Cassell (1996) refers to Thornberg's (1994) three phases which represent a company's evolution towards a more diverse heterogeneous culture:

1. bring in more women and minorities;
2. emphasise working on understanding how people are different and why, by concentrating on problems of individual and group behaviour associated with race and gender;
3. focus on company culture which involves evaluating all of the organis-ation's procedures and policies.

Based on their research findings of 'black' managers in the US, Dickens and Dickens (1991) strongly propose that organisations adopt the management of diversity and train and develop their managers to use multicultural management, thereby learning to comprehend the gender and ethnic differences that give added value to all employees: 'The different ingredients in a salad are mixed together, but they are not blended; each piece keeps its own texture, flavour, and colour, i.e. its own integrity' (Dickens and Dickens, 1991). The British African and Caribbean Finance Forum *et al.* (1996) emphasised the lack of multicultural management education in both general management education courses and management development. They referred to recent reviews which found little evidence of systematic integration of equal opportunities issues in management education course curricula.

Certainly, the introduction of effective management of diversity in organisations was a recommendation repeated time and time again by the black and ethnic minority women managers interviewed, as typified by the following statement: 'Cultural diversity in organisations has got to be advantageous. Without it, individuals suffer – organisations suffer. Not only that, organisational diversity reflects positively on the community as a whole and companies have moral responsibilities to the multiracial society in which we now all live.'

BLACK AND ETHNIC MINORITY WORKERS AND TRADE UNIONS

With union representation being associated with better pay, job benefits and opportunities, the under-representation of women in unions (particularly those working part time) acts as a major disadvantage for women workers (Davidson, 1996). Historically, trade unions have been predominantly male domains. However, in recent years there has been increased participation of women in trade unions, at membership, office-holder and executive levels. In 1995, 35% of male employees were union members compared with 30% of women. Furthermore, whereas there was little variability in union membership among men by educational qualifications, twice as many women with some post-school training or education, but without a degree (58%), were in a union, compared with women with no qualifications (24%). What is also interesting to note is that a higher percentage of British 'black' employees (41%) are union members compared to white employees (32%). Just under one in five of Pakistani/Bangladeshi employees are union members compared to 28% of Indian workers. Nevertheless, the differences in industry density of union membership among whites and other ethnic groups is very small (31%) (EOR, 1996).

On the whole, women are less likely to be union members than men and unlike white women, 'black' women are less likely to be represented in the trades union structure (Bhavnani, 1994). Jones' (1993) study revealed that the highest rates of trade union membership were for Afro-Caribbean women at 41% which compares to 33% for African women, 32% for Indian, with Chinese, Pakistani and African Asian women having the lowest rates. Recent reports have emphasised the lack of confidence 'black' union members have felt in the ability of unions to protect their interests, often through fear of losing white support (Mirza, 1992). Obviously, unions need to address this issue and also monitor their effectiveness, particularly taking into account Bhavnani's (1994) evaluation when she stated: 'But whilst the 1992 study of 10 unions for the TUC showed that some unions had made attempts to develop links with women's and race committees, no systematic attempts have been made to monitor effectively' (Labour Research Department, 1993).

RACE AND EQUAL OPPORTUNITIES – CHANGING THE LAW

The Race Relations Act 1976 states that racial discrimination is unlawful. Following Parliamentary approval in 1983, the Race Relations Code of Practice in Employment came into operation in April 1984. Under the Race Relations Act 1976, the Code is admissible in evidence in any proceedings before an industrial tribunal and industrial tribunals are no longer constrained by limits on the awards they can make to victims of discrimination. CRE (1995) have illustrated that the cost of discrimination is high for organisations in terms of poor staff morale, loss of reputation and money. In 1990–91 for example, the financial cost to employers of responding to cases of sex and racial discrimination was about £5 million (Tremlett and Banerji, 1992).

The question one must ask about equal opportunities for ethnic minority women at work, is whether it should be severely legislated. Should European countries adopt the US approach of 'affirmative action', whereby organisations which receive government grants, loans or contracts must follow a positive recruitment strategy towards the employment of minority groups or lose their government award?

In the final analysis, if the position of black and ethnic minority women at work and in management in particular, is to improve there needs to be stronger legislative programmes to force compliance with the principles and realities of race and equal opportunities. Almost all the interview sample of black and ethnic minority women managers asserted that there should be stronger legislation and government action to fight racism. Most were in favour of positive action programmes which focused on racial, as well as gender and disability issues. Some of the women managers were also in favour of legally enforced affirmative action programmes although there was concern voiced about possible 'backlashes', and the dangers of inappropriate appointments based on skin colour rather than ability. For example, one of our middle female managers proclaimed: 'The law definitely isn't tight enough. In addition, CRE does not have enough powers. We need more action and less words.' Another, more senior female Afro-Caribbean executive exclaimed:

> From my experience in the US, if it's not implemented properly, legal affirmative action tends to get people's backs up and this can make it even more difficult for black people. I would not want to be promoted or given a job *because* I was black. However, for some (black) people I acknowledge its probably the only way they could progress in some organisations so it would be good for them. It's a difficult one, this.

Some felt the legal system needed to be tightened and strengthened throughout numerous systems:

> The legal structures to fight harassment and discrimination need to be improved and better implemented. Social security laws, education, training, social provisions – anything which maintains unequal access to equality of opportunity – particularly for ethnic minorities – needs to be changed and challenged.

A few believed their views towards affirmative action had mellowed following their own personal experiences in the workplace: 'I'm much more open towards the introduction of affirmative action than I used to be. I can't help thinking that without it, if we continue the way we are, we'll (black women) be no further on in ten years time. In fact, I'm certain of it.' Personally, the author agrees with this statement, having followed the extremely slow progression of white women managers over the past two decades without the aid of affirmative action legislation in the UK. Although American researchers such as Dickens and Dickens (1991) make strong assertions such as 'Affirmative action is almost a dead issue. This is the age of diversity', they do acknowledge that affirmative action had been most successful in forcing US organisations to open up job and career opportunities to minorities that would have otherwise remained blocked. What is needed in Britain is for us to learn from the American experience and delicately combine the successful facets of both affirmative action policy and diversity management models. Properly implemented, legislative affirmative action policies can successfully ensure the increase in numbers of minority groups into management and other areas of employment without them being 'assimilated'. Affirmative action does not have to result in these minority groups being part of the 'white organisational, cultural melting pot', if the principles and strategies associated with the management of diversity are adopted simultaneously.

OUR CHILDREN, THE FUTURE AND CHANGING
SOCIETAL ATTITUDES

At the end of every interview, each of the black and ethnic minority female managers were invited to state whether there were any other issues they wanted to raise. At this point, many of them spoke with great passion about the future prospects for their children and their hopes for changes in societal attitudes, particularly in relation to how black and ethnic minority people are portrayed in the media. The majority felt that the media tended to be very negative:

> The ways the media selects, views and reports black people is usually quite negative, whether it be the way Afro-Caribbean's are portrayed in drama or how news issues cover Third World issues. Often it's black images when programmes cover teenage pregnancies or children not doing well at school. There are few positive images in mainstream television on such programmes as *The Bill* or *Eastenders*.

A few women highlighted the television and film industry's habit of linking black women with seduction and sex and rarely as role models for career women or heroines:

> We are not portrayed as being strong characters. I don't like the fact that we are often portrayed as prostitutes.

> Black women are still seen as images of 'the unknown' – often with a seductive element – rather than positive career women for instance. In a lot of newspapers, magazines and films, it's always the white woman who is the heroine, the one selling the cars, etc.

Some women expressed feelings of deprivation and feeling invisible in what is supposedly, a multicultural society:

> We feel starved of seeing our own reflection on TV. In fact, its common for us to ring each other up if there's a programme with a positive image of a black woman in it – it happens so rarely.

> In Jamaica, black people are everywhere – on a packet of Daz even. Here, you never see yourself.

In Hooks (1990) analysis of negative media images of 'black' women in the US, she contends that the exclusion of 'black' women by the whites who control the media, is to emphasise their undesirability either as friends or as sexual partners. Furthermore, she proposes that this also reinforces the concept that 'black' men but not 'black' women, are accepted. Here 'black' women are seen as a threat to the existing race–sex hierarchy. In the words of Hook (1990):

> Negative images of black women in television and film are not simply impressed upon the psyches of white males, they affect all Americans. Black mothers and fathers constantly complain that television lowers the self-confidence and self-esteem of black girls. Even on television commercials the

black female child is rarely visible largely because sexist–racist Americans tend to see the black male as the representative of the black race. So commercials and advertisements in magazines may portray a white female and male but feel that it is enough to have a black male to represent black people. The same logic occurs in regular television programs.

Some of the most moving and emotional experiences related by the black and ethnic minority women interviewees concerned their battles, grief and sorrow, when their children experienced racism. For one women manager, her preschool child was already being exposed to covert racism; she described her complex feelings of despair and determination:

> I can't see things changing. I keep battling, but the power base is in the hands of people who don't get the opportunity to meet (black) people, who aren't like them. Then you get the average *Sun* reader, who uses racist language all the time. My son goes to a nursery school where if you are good you get a star – if you are bad – you get a *black* dot. He comes home and says 'mummy, I've got a black dot'! I know the teacher couldn't even cope if I brought the subject up – she'd burst into tears. They once inferred to him that he wasn't black (i.e. you're not different). Or the teachers would say to him 'oh dear, you've got a black man's pinch' – when he'd hurt his hand. I'd never even heard of that expression. They never even stop to think there is anything wrong with what they're doing or saying – no hesitation or thought ever.

A recent report by the British charity ChildLine revealed that a large proportion of ethnic minority youngsters are still suffering blatant racial harassment and bullying on a daily basis. This is particularly prevalent for ethnic minority children in predominantly white schools. In response to this report, the *Guardian* (1996) quoted Herman Ouseley, Chairman of the Commission of Racial Equality, who said that it reminded him of his childhood experiences in the 1950s: 'For too many young people, growing up in Britain today means facing racially motivated violence and persistent racial discrimination' (the *Guardian*, 1996). Certainly, this was clearly evident by the following painful stories recounted by two mothers interviewed:

> I travel to America a lot and there, racism is more 'black and white'. In a way, I'd rather it be that way – people there say what they feel and its easier to cope with. You know where you stand. Here, racism is a much greyer area. People don't often even like admitting it exists. I can cope with it myself now, but you do feel the pain when it touches your children. My daughter did law and was brilliant. However, when it came to training to be a barrister – no one, and I mean *no one*, would take her on. She was warned that law wasn't the place to get on if you were female and Asian. She was determined though but I know this hurt her. She's a law lecturer now and says she likes it, but deep down, I feel she wishes she were now a barrister. I think its particularly hard for her when she meets white colleagues who did law with her – many of whom are now practising barristers.
>
> My son had similar experiences. He went to a private school to do his A-levels. He was very brilliant and wanted to do medicine. However, his school

suggested he should be a nurse and wrote him poor prediction reports to the universities he applied for. He got excellent A-levels but had not managed to secure a place at a good university because of his poor school references. He eventually ended up at Oxford and is now a top Medical Consultant.

My son and daughter have both recently hit racial prejudice at school. My daughter is a brilliant musician but they wouldn't help her progress – eventually she had to turn to America and was awarded a music scholarship, so she's there now studying cello.

My son was the only black student at his school. He was the best athlete in the school, got excellent O- and A-levels. He'd set his heart on one of the school's scholarships to Oxford but the school refused to put him forward for one. My son was devastated, he couldn't believe it – one of the best athletes and academically brilliant. I went to see the Head to challenge his decision and he said to me – 'you can take me to court if you like – but we've got more money to fight you, than you've got – and we'll win!

My son's left school and got a job. He'll go to university eventually, but he needs time to get over it. I'm letting him work it out himself – I'm always here for him to help him if he needs me.

In her writings on African-American families in white communities, Tatum (1997) concludes that most, if not all 'black' parents struggle with these issues. For some 'black' families, the 'black' community can sometimes act as a buffer between the child and the negative messages of the dominant white society. When this buffer is not accessible, African-American families need to find their own means for addressing their children's racial socialisation. According to Tatum (1997): 'The stress of trying to find the right balance between protecting children from the pain of racism and inoculating them against what will probably be unavoidable encounters, is part of daily living for these families.'

On a more optimistic note, a number of black and ethnic minority women interviewed viewed the very fact that they had secured prominent managerial jobs, gave them *power* to ensure changes for their children and for the future of black and ethnic minority women managers of tomorrow – by acting as important role models:

I see a brighter future for my daughter – the culture and opportunities are changing.

I've brought her up in an environment where black women are seen as strong, supportive and successful. I'm already working on getting a black mentor for my 11 year old. I've got a black teacher who does private teaching with my daughter at home. I also take my daughter into work to let her get the feel of it.

Whatever field of work you are in, you must make opportunities for your children – they'll need your help. I actively act as a role model for my daughter – she already says she wants to do my job.

Black women in management act as important role models encouraging future generations of black women to move forward and upward into management.

CONCLUSIONS

One must recognise from the material presented in this book, that the multiplicity of experience and discrimination encountered by black and ethnic minority women managers is complex and varied dependent on gender, class and specific ethnic origin. This was nicely phrased by Bhavnani (1994) when she said:

> Whilst black women's experience is specific and differentiated, it should not always be assumed to be *constantly* different from white women or black men. There will be similarities as well as differences depending on the contexts. Differences within the categories of black, of women and class need to be understood within the commonality. This does not mean that the effects of 'race' discrimination should be 'added' on to sex discrimination which, in turn, is 'added' on to class discrimination. But as well as recognising specificity of experience, there needs to be an appreciation of the operation of the multiplicity of discrimination.

There is a need for further qualitative and quantitative action research carried out by researchers from various ethnic groups, to further investigate and compare the experiences of both female and male managers from different ethnic backgrounds.

In the final analysis, one cannot rely solely on legalistic approaches to equal rights for black and ethnic minority women managers, but must hope that individuals, organisations and governments can work together and help *'smash the concrete ceiling'*. By the year 2000, the majority of new employees entering the workforce will be women and ethnic minorities, particularly highly educated black and ethnic minority women. These changes need to be urgently acknowledged and this was aptly voiced by one of the interview sample when she stated:

> Rather than Equal Opportunity Policies, what is needed is Positive Action. There have been quota systems for white male managers for centuries, but no-one calls that discrimination.

Appendix

CRE (1995) Checklist when Considering, Planning and Implementing a Racial Equality Programme

COMMITMENT

- Does the organisation have a written racial equality policy, or a section on racial equality within an equal opportunity policy, clearly linked to the organisation's aims and objectives?
- Is there a clear public commitment at the highest level of the organisation, emphasising the value placed on equality of opportunity?
- Does the organisation communicate the policy and programme to:
  - employees and their representatives, where applicable;
  - applicants and potential applicants;
  - customers and clients;
  - shareholders;
  - suppliers of goods and services;
  - external organisations, such as Training and Enterprise Councils (or Local Enterprise Companies in Scotland), etc.;
  - the public?
- Does the organisation have an action plan covering:
  - the role of senior management;
  - who is responsible for implementing the policy;
  - resources needed to make changes;
  - objectives and targets, and who is accountable;
  - timetables and time scales;
  - methods of measuring progress;
  - consultation with: all staff and employee representatives; groups and institutions in the wider community, including ethnic minority organisations;
  - the role of line managers, and local or devolved units;
  - the rights and responsibilities of individual employees?

ACTION

- Does the organisation collect information by ethnic origin on:
  - key areas of personnel practice;
  - staff in post;
  - applicants;
  - the labour market;
  - users of services and customers, through market profiles?
- Does the organisation use this information to analyse:
  - the current position;
  - the effects of the organisation's employment practices on different ethnic groups, and the reasons for these effects;
  - gaps in the goods or services provided, and the reasons for these;
  - what objectives and targets to set?
- Does the organisation, as an employer, review the following in detail:
  - recruitment channels;
  - job criteria against the requirements of the job;
  - selection methods, including tests, against required performance;
  - training needs;
  - promotion routes and procedures;
  - disciplinary action;
  - staff appraisals;
  - selection for dismissal, redundancy, transfer or redeployment?
- Does the organisation, as a purchaser and provider of goods and services, review the following in detail:
  - its purchasing policy – giving ethnic minority-led businesses a fair chance; setting standards for contractors where this is legally permitted;
  - its marketing plans – reaching all sections of the community?
- Does the organisation conduct detailed overall reviews of:
  - its progress in achieving objectives;
  - its action plans, including targets, objectives, and timetables?
- Has the organisation introduced or reviewed policies and procedures covering:
  - racial harassment or victimisation;
  - grievances;
  - disciplinary matters;
  - health and safety (taking account of language and cultural factors);
  - dismissal;
  - redundancy;
  - transfer or redeployment?
- Does the organisation provide training on the action programme for:
  - managers;
  - human resources or personnel managers and equal opportunity staff;
  - recruitment and selection personnel;

- trainers;
- other staff involved in the programme?
- Does the organisation encourage ethnic minority staff to develop particular skills in areas where they are under-represented? For example, by using:
  - targeted training;
  - support systems.
- Does the organisation include ethnic minority communities in its business and community links or in its programme of corporate citizenship? For example activities such as:
  - links with schools, universities and colleges, community groups, etc.;
  - work experience opportunities such as external mentoring or shadowing schemes;
  - cooperating with other employers in developing and sharing good practice, such as local employers' equal opportunities networks;
  - pre-employment training schemes;
  - sponsoring awards or bursaries for individuals from ethnic minority groups, where this is legally permitted;
  - encouraging ethnic minority-led businesses to tender for contracts;
  - sponsorship of ethnic minority community projects?

OUTCOMES

- Has the organisation, as an employer, been able to show, for example, that:
  - it has removed unfair barriers to entry and progress in the organisation;
  - it has attracted staff from diverse backgrounds;
  - there is a better understanding of race issues among staff and greater appreciation of the advantages of diversity;
  - ethnic minority staff feel more appreciated;
  - staff are more confident about expressing their views and concerns because they know they will be heard;
  - it has a reputation as a good employer, and attracts diverse applicants;
  - there is a good atmosphere at work because the harassment policy and procedures are effective, and staff know their rights and responsibilities;
  - recruitment and other selection is more cost-effective, because of lower staff turnover;
  - grievances are fewer, or dealt with more effectively?
- Has the organisation, as a supplier or purchaser of goods or services, been able to show, for example, that:
  - it has more ethnic minority customers and clients;
  - sales or services to minority groups in the UK have improved;

- – international contacts and sales have increased;
- – it has persuaded other employers to develop effective equal opportunity policies?
- Has the organisation, as a corporate citizen, been able to show, for example, that:
  - – there is more goodwill towards it among all the local communities;
  - – it gets favourable publicity;
  - – it is widely recognised as an active participant in the community;
  - – it is becoming known as an organisation with a genuine commitment to racial equality?

Source: CRE (1995) reproduced here with permission

References

African and Caribbean Finance Forum, Foundation for Management Education and The Wainwright Trust (1996) *The Cement Roof: Afro-Caribbean People in Management*, London: Midland Bank.

Anderson, M.L. (1993) Studying Across Difference: Race, Class and Gender in Qualitative Research, in J.H. Stansfield and R.M. Dennis (Eds) *Race and Ethnicity in Research Methods*, London: Sage, pp. 39–52.

Arnold, V. and Davidson, M.J. (1990) Adopt A Mentor – The New Way Ahead for Women Managers, *Women in Management Review and Abstracts*, 5(1), pp. 10–18.

Australian Bureau of Statistics (1992) *The Labour Force, Australia*, July, Cat. No. 6203–0.

Aziz, S. (1995) The Global Entrepreneur, Paper presented to the Researching Asian Entrepreneurship Conference, 9 November.

Bakshi, P. (1992) *Small Business Intervention Strategies and Ethnic Minority/Migrant Women*, Birmingham: School of Continuing Studies, University of Birmingham.

Bass, B.M., Avolio B.J. and Atwater, L. (1996) Transformational Leadership of Men and Women, *Applied Psychology: An International Review*, 45.

Bell, E.L. (1990) The Bicultural Life Experience of Career-Oriented Black Women, *Journal of Organizational Behaviour*, 11(6), pp. 459–78.

Bell, E.L., Denton, T. and Nkomo, S. (1993) Women of Colour in Management: Towards an Inclusive Analysis, in E. Fagenson (Ed) *Women in Management: Trends, Issues and Challenges in Managerial Diversity, Vol. 4, Women and Work: A Research Policy Series*, Newbury Park, CA: Sage, pp. 105–30.

Bell, E.L., and Nkomo, S.M. (1992) Re-Visioning Women Managers' Lives, in A.J. Mills and P. Tancred (Eds) *Gendering Organizational Analysis*, London: Sage.

Betters-Reed, B. and Moore, L. (1995) Shifting the Management Development Paradigm for Women, *Journal of Management Development*, 14(2), pp. 24–38.

Bhavnani, R. (1994) *Black Women in The Labour Market – A Research Review*, Manchester: Equal Opportunities Commission.

Bravette, G. (1994) *Black Women Managers and Participating Action Research*, Published Conference Paper in World Congress on American Learning, Action Research and Process Management, University of Bath.

Brenner, O.C., Tomkiewicz, J. and Schein, V.E. (1989) The Relationship Between Sex Role Stereotypes and Requisite Management Characteristics Revisited, *Academy of Management Journal*, 32, pp. 662–69.

Briscoe, G. and Wilson, R.A. (1992) Forecasting Economic Activity Rates, *International Journal of Forecasting*, 8, pp. 201–17.

Case, S. (1993) Wide-Verbal-Repertoire-Speech-Gender, Language and Managerial Influence, *Women's Studies International Forum*, 16(3), pp. 271–90.

Case, S. (1994) Gender Differences in Communication and Behaviour in Organisations, in M.J. Davidson and R.J. Burke (Eds) *Women in Management: Current Research Issues*, London: Paul Chapman, pp. 144–67.

Cassell, C. (1996) A Fatal Attraction? Strategic HRM and the Business Case for Women's Progression at Work, *Personnel Review*, 25(5), pp. 51–66.

City College Manchester (1995) *Mentor Service*, Manchester: City College.

Clarke, L.W. (1986) Women Supervisors Experience Sexual Harassment Too, *Supervisory Management*, 31, pp. 35–6.

Cleveland, J.N. (1994) Women and Sexual Harassment: Work and Well-Being in US Organisations, in M.J. Davidson and R. Burke (Eds) *Women in Management – Current Research Issues*, London: Paul Chapman, pp. 168–91.

Clutterbuck, D. and Devine, M. (Eds) (1987) *Business Women – Present and Future*, London: Macmillan.

Collins, P.H. (1991) *Black Feminist Thought – Knowledge, Consciousness and the Politics of Empowerment*, Perspectives on Gender, Vol.2, London: Routledge.

Cooper, C.L., Cooper, R. and Eaker, L.H. (1988) *Living With Stress*, London: Penguin.

Cooper, C.L. and Melhuish, A. (1984) Executive Stress and Health: Differences Between Men and Women, *Journal of Occupational Medicine*, 26(2), pp. 99–103.

Cox, C. and Cooper, C.L. (1988) *High Flyers*, Oxford: Basil Blackwell.

Cox, J. (1993) *Cultural Diversity in Organizations: Theory, Research and Practice*, San Francisco: Berrett-Koehler Publishers.

Cox, T.C. (1990) Problems With Research by Organizational Scholars on Issues of Race and Ethnicity, *Journal of Applied Behavioural Science*, 26(1), pp. 5–23.

Cox, T. and Nkomo, S.M. (1990) Invisible Men and Women: A Status Report on Race as a Variable in Organization Behaviour Research, *Journal of Organizational Behaviour*, 11(6), pp. 419–32.

CRE (1995) *Racial Equality Means Business – A Standard for Racial Equality for Employers*, London: CRE.

Davidson, M.J. (1996) Women and Employment, in P. Warr (Ed) *Psychology at Work*, London: Penguin, pp. 279–307.

Davidson, M.J. and Burke, R. (Eds) (1994) *Women in Management – Current Research Issues*, London: Paul Chapman.

Davidson, M.J. and Cooper, C.L. (1982) *High Pressure – Working Lives of Women Managers*, London: Fontana.

Davidson, M.J. and Cooper, C.L. (1983) *Stress and The Woman Manager*, Oxford: Martin Robertson.

Davidson, M.J. and Cooper, C.L. (1986) Executive Women Under Pressure, *International Review of Applied Psychology*, 35, pp. 301–26.

Davidson, M.J. and Cooper, C.L. (1987) Female Managers in Britain – A Comparative Review, *Human Resource Management*, 26, pp. 217–42.

Davidson, M.J. and Cooper, C.L. (1992) *Shattering The Glass Ceiling – The Woman Manager*, London: Paul Chapman.

Davidson, M.J. and Cooper, C.L. (Eds) (1993) *European Women in Business and Management*, London: Paul Chapman.

Davidson, M.J., Cooper, C.L. and Baldini, V. (1995) Occupational Stress in Female and Male Graduate Managers – A Comparative Study, *Stress Medicine*, 11, pp. 157–75.

Deakins, D., Majmudar, M. and Paddison, A. (1996) Success Factors for Ethnic Minorities in Business, Paper presented at the 19th ISBA National Small Firms' Policy and Research Conference, Birmingham.

Denton, T.C. (1990) Bonding and Supportive Relationships Among Black Professional Women: Rituals of Restoration, *Journal of Organisational Behaviour*, 11(6), pp. 447–58.

Devanna, M.A. (1987) Women in Management: Progress and Promise, *Human Resource Management*, 26, pp. 409–81.

Department for Education and Employment (1996) *One Year On – Implementing the Global Platform for Action from the UN Fourth World Conference on Women*, London: DEE.

Department for Education and Employment (1997) *Separate Tables – Statistics on Women and Men in Education, Training and Employment*, London: DEE.

Dickens, F. and Dickens, J.B. (1991) *The Black Manager – Making It In The Corporate World*, New York: American Management Association.

Discoll, M.P. and Cooper, C.L. (1996) Sources and Management of Executive Job Stress and Burnout, in P. Warr (Ed) *Psychology at Work*, London: Penguin, pp. 188–223.

Doyle, J.A. and Paludi, M.A. (1995) *Sex and Gender – The Human Experience*, Dubuquiee, IA USA: Brown and Benchmark.

Earnshaw, J. and Davidson, M.J. (1994) Redefining Sexual Harassment Via Industrial Tribunal Claims – An Investigation of the Legal and Psychosocial Process, *Personnel Review*, 23(8), pp. 3–16.

The Economist (1996a) Breaking The Glass Ceiling, 10 August, p.15.

The Economist (1996b) Women in American Boardrooms – Through A Glass, Darkly, 10 August, p.60.

Elkin, A. and Rosch, P. (1990) Promoting Mental Health at the Workplace: The Prevention Side of Stress Management, *Occupational Medicine: State of the Art Review*, 5, pp. 739–54.

EOR (1996) Union Membership Higher Among Blacks Than Whites, *Equal Opportunities Review*, 68, July/August, pp. 4–5.

Epstein, C.F. (1973) Positive Effects of the Multiple Negative: Explaining the Success of Black Professional Women, *American Journal of Sociology*, 78(4), pp. 912–35.

Essed, P. (1991) *Understanding Everyday Racism – An Interdisciplinary Theory*, London: Sage.

Evans, K.M. and Herr, E.L. (1991) The Influence of Racism and Sexism in the Career Development of African American Women, *Journal of Multicultural Counselling and Development*, July, 19, pp. 130–35.

Fagenson, E.A. (1989) The Mentor Advantage: Perceived Career/Job Experiences of Protégés Versus Non-Protégés, *Journal of Organizational Behaviour*, 10, pp. 309–20.

Feagin, J.R. (1992) On Not Taking Gendered Racism Seriously: The Failure of the Mass Media and the Social Sciences, *The Journal of Applied Behavioural Science*, 28(3), September, pp. 400–6.

Fernandez, J.P. (1981) *Racism and Sexism in Corporate Life*, Lexington MA: Lexington Books.

Fitzgerald, L.F. (1986) On the Essential Relations Between Education and Work, *Journal of Vocational Behaviour*, 28, pp. 254–84.

Ford, D.L. and Wells, L. (1985) Upward Mobility Factors Among Black Public Administrators: The Role of Mentors, *Centerboard: Journal of the Center for Human Relations*, 3(1), pp. 33–48.

French, J.R.P. and Caplan, R.D. (1970) Psychosocial Factors in Coronary Heart Disease, *Industrial Medicine*, 39, pp. 383–97.

Frone, M.R., Russell, M. and Cooper, M.L. (1990) Occupational Stressors, Psychological Resources and Psychological Distress: A Comparison of Black and White Workers, Paper presented at the Annual Meeting of the Academy of Management, San Francisco.

Fulbright, K. (1986) The Myth of the Double Advantage: Black Female Managers, *Review of the Black Political Economy*, Fall/Winter, 1985–86, 4(2–3), pp. 33–45.

Gilkes, C.T. (1990) Liberated to Work Like Dogs: Labelling Black Women and their work, in H.Y. Grossman and N.L. Chester (Eds) *The Experience and Meaning of Work in Women's Lives,* London: Lawrence Erlbaum, pp. 165–88.

Gooden, W. (1981) The Adult Development of Black Men, Unpublished Doctoral Dissertation, Yale University.

Greenglass, E.R. (1990) Type A Behaviour, Career Aspirations and Role Conflict in Professional Women, *Journal of Social Behaviour and Personality*, 5, pp. 307–22.

Greenglass, E.R. (1995) An Interactional Perspective on Job Related Stress in Managerial Women, *The Southern Psychologist*, 21, pp. 42–8.

Greenhaus, J.H., Parasuraman, S. and Wormley, W.M. (1990) Effects of Race on Organizational Experiences, Job Performance Evaluations and Career Outcomes, *Academy of Management Journal*, 33(1), pp. 64–86.

The *Guardian* (1996) Ethnic Minority Children 'Still Suffer Racism Today', 23 July, p. 6.

Gutek, B.A. (1985) *Sex and The Workplace*, San Francisco: Jossey Bass.

Hansard Society Commission (1990) *Women at The Top*, Hansard Society.

Harnett, O. and Novarra, V. (1979) Facilitating the Entry of Women into Management Posts, Paper presented at Association of Teachers of Management Conference, The Training and Development Needs of Women Managers, November, London.

Haynes, S.G. and Feinleib, M. (1980) Women, Work and Coronary Heart Disease: Heart Study, *American Journal of Public Health*, 70, pp. 133–41.

Hede, A. (1995) Managerial Inequity in the Australian Workforce: A Longitudinal Analysis, *International Review of Women and Leadership*, 1(1), pp. 11–21.

Herbert, J. (1989) *Black Entrepreneurs and Adult Development*, New York: Praeger Press.

Higginbotham, E. and Weber, L. (1992) Moving Up with Kin and Community – Upward Social Mobility for Black and White Women, *Gender and Society*, 6(3), pp. 416–40.

Hirsh, W. and Bevan, S. (1988) *What Makes A Manager? In Search of a Language for Management Skills, IMS Report No. 144*, University of Sussex: Institute of Manpower Studies.

Hirsh, W. and Jackson, C. (1989) *Women Into Management – Issues Influencing the Entry of Women Into Management Jobs, Paper No. 158*, University of Sussex: Institute of Manpower Studies.

Hisrich, R.D. and Brush, C. (1987) Women Entrepreneurs: A Longitudinal Study, in *Frontiers of Entrepreneurship Research*, Proceedings of the 7th Annual Babson

College Entrepreneurship Research Conference, USA, NC: Churchill.

Hite, L.M. (1996) Black Women Managers and Administrators: Experiences and Implications, *Women in Management Review*, 11(6), pp. 11–17.

HMSO (1991) *British Social Attitudes Survey*, London: HMSO.

HMSO (1995) *Social Focus on Women*, London: HMSO.

Holder, J. (1995) Challenging Racism: The BBC Mentor Scheme, in C. Itzin and J. Newman (Eds) *Gender, Culture and Organizational Change*, London: Routledge, pp. 171–81.

Hooks, B. (1990) *Ain't I A Woman – Black Women and Feminism*, London: Pluto Press.

Horner, M.S. (1972) Toward An Understanding of Achievement Related Conflicts in Women, *Journal of Social Issues*, 2(2), pp. 157–75.

Iles, P. and Auluck, R. (1991) The Experience of Black Workers, in M. Davidson and J. Earnshaw (Eds) *Vulnerable Workers – Psychosocial and Legal Issues*, London: Wiley, pp. 297–322.

Institute of Management (1992) *The Key to the Men's Club*, Bristol: I.M. Books.

Institute of Management and Remuneration Economics (1995) *UK National Management Survey*, London: Institute of Management.

Institute of Management and Remuneration Economics (1996) *UK National Management Survey*, London: Institute of Management.

James, K. (1994) Social Identity, Work Stress, and Minority Workers' Health, in G.P. Keita and J.J. Hurrell (Eds) *Job Stress in A Changing Workforce – Investigating Gender, Diversity and Family Issues*, Washington: American Psychological Association, pp. 127–46.

James, K., Lovato, C. and Khoo, G. (1994) Social Identity Correlates of Minority Workers Health, *Academy of Management Journal*, 37(2), pp. 383–91.

Jones, T. (1993) *Britain's Ethnic Minorities*, London: Policy Studies Institute.

Kagan, J. and Moss, H.A. (1962) *Birth to Maturity*, New York: Wiley.

Kandola, R. and Fullerton, J. (1994) *Managing the Mosaic: Diversity in Action*, London: IPD.

Kanter, R. (1977) *Men and Women of the Corporation*, New York: Basic Books.

Labour Force Survey (1995) London: HMSO.

Labour Market Trends (1996) London: HMSO.

Labour Research Department (1993) *Black Works and Trade Unions: An LRD Guide*, London: LRD.

Lach, D.H. and Gwartney-Gibbs, P.A. (1993) Sociological Perspectives on Sexual Harassment and Workplace Dispute Resolution, *Journal of Vocational Behaviour*, 42, pp. 102–15.

Lakoff, R. (1975) *Language and Women's Place*, New York: Harper and Row.

LARRIE (1995) *What's New*, LARRIE Quarterly Update, No. 5, March.

Larwood, L. and Wood, M.M. (1977) *Women in Management*, London: Lexington Books.

Lennox Birch, E. (1994) *Black American Women's Writing – A Quilt of Many Colours*, London: Harvester Wheatsheaf.

Lownes, S.N. (1994) Summer Quarter Update, July, Croydon: Management Computerisation Data Base.

Malone, B. (1981) Relationship of Black Female Administrators' Mentoring Experiences and Career Satisfaction, Unpublished Doctoral Dissertation, University of Cincinnati.

Margolis, B., Kroes, W. and Quinn, R. (1974) Job Stress: An Unlisted Occupational Hazard, *Journal of Occupational Medicine*, 1, pp. 659–61.

Marshall, A. (1994) Sensuous Sapphires: A Study of the Social Construction of Black Female Sexuality, in M. Maynard and J. Purvis (Eds) *Researching Women's Lives From a Feminist Perspective*, London: Taylor and Francis, pp. 106–24.

Marshall, J. (1994) Why Women Leave Senior Management Jobs: My Research Approach and Some Initial Findings, in M. Tantan (Ed) *Women in Management: The Second Wave*, London: Routledge Press, pp. 4–5.

Marshall, J. (1995) *Women Managers – Moving On*, London: Routledge Press.

Mayor, V. (1996) Investing in People: Personal and Professional Development of Black Nurses, *Health Visitor*, 69(1), January, pp. 20–3.

Melamed, T. (1995) Barriers to Women's Career Success: Human Capital, Career Choices, Structural Determinants, or Simply Sex Discrimination, *Applied Psychology – An International Review*, 44(4), pp. 295–314.

Mentor Training Services (1995) *New Mentor Pack*, London: Mentor Training Services.

Mirza, H.S. (1992) *Young, Female and Black*, London: Routledge.

Murray, M. (1982) The Middle Years of Life of Middle Class Black Men: An Exploratory Study, Unpublished Doctoral Dissertation, University of Cincinnati.

New Earnings Survey (1996) London: HMSO.

Nicholson, N. and West, M.A. (1988) *Managerial Job Change: Men and Women in Transition*, Cambridge: Cambridge University Press.

Nkomo, S.M. (1988) Race and Sex: The Forgotten Case of the Black Female Manager, in S. Rose and L. Larwood (Ed) *Women's Careers – Pathways and Pitfalls*, London: Praeger.

Opportunity 2000 (1995) *Opportunity 2000: Fourth Year Report*, London.

Opportunity 2000 (1996) *Opportunity 2000: Fifth Year Report*, London.

Owen, D. (1994) *Ethnic Minority Women and the Labour Market: Analysis of the 1991 Census*, Manchester: Equal Opportunities Commission.

Plantenga, J. (1995) Labour-Market Participation of Women in the European Union, in A. van Doorne-Huiskes, J. van Hoot and E. Ruelofs (Eds) *Women and the European Labour Markets*, London: Paul Chapman, pp. 1–14.

Popeau, J. (1995) *Black Teachers Mentoring Scheme*, London: Goldsmiths, University of London.

Powell, G.N. (1988) *Women and Men in Management*, London: Sage.

Ram, M. and Barr, P. (1997) Supporting Ethnic Minority Enterprise: Views From the Providers, in M. Ram, D. Deakins and D. Smallbone (Eds) *Small Firms*, London: Paul Chapman (forthcoming).

Reid, T.P. (1984) Feminism Versus Minority Group Identity: Not For Black Women Only, *Sex Roles*, 10(3/4), pp. 247–55.

Reskin, B. and Padovic, I. (1994) *Women and Men at Work*, Pine: Forge Press, USA.

Roberts, C., Davies, E. and Jupp, T. (1992) *Language and Discrimination, A Study of Communication in Multi-Ethnic Workplaces*, London: Longman.

Rosener, J.B. (1990) Ways Women Lead, *Harvard Business Review*, November–December, pp. 119–25.

Rosenman, R.H., Friedman, M. and Strauss, R. (1966) CHD in the Western Collaborative Group Study, *Journal of the American Medical Association*, 195, pp. 86–92.

Rubenstein, M. (1988) *The Dignity of Women at Work: A Report on the Problem of*

Sexual Harassment in the Member States of the European Communities, COMV/4121087, Luxembourg: Office for Official Publications of the European Communities.

Rubenstein, M. (1991) Devising a Sexual Harassment Policy, *Personnel Management*, February, pp. 8–10.

Rubery, J. and Fagan, C. (1993) *Bulletin on Women and Employment in the European Commission*, Brussels: European Commission.

Rubery, J., Fagan, C. and Grimshaw, D. (1994) *Bulletin on Women and Employment in the EU, (No. 5)*, Brussels: European Commission.

Scase, R. and Goffee, R. (1989) *Redundant Managers: Their Work and Life Style*, London: Unwin Hyman.

Schein, V.E. (1994) Managerial Sex Typing: A Persistent and Pervasive Barrier to Women's Opportunities, in M.J. Davidson and R.J. Burke (Eds) *Women in Management – Current Research Issues*, London: Paul Chapman, pp. 41–52.

Schein, V.E. and Davidson, M.J. (1993) Think Manager – Think Male, *Management Development Review*, 6(3), pp. 24–8.

Schein, V.E. and Mueller, R. (1992) Sex Role Stereotyping and Requisite Management Characteristics: A Cross Cultural Look, *Journal of Organizational Behaviour*, 13(5), pp. 439–47.

Schein, V.E., Mueller, R. and Jacobson, C. (1989) The Relationship Between Sex Role Stereotypes and Requisite Management Characteristics Among College Students, *Sex Roles*, 20, pp. 103–10.

Simpson, G. (1984) The Daughters of Charlotte Ray: The Career Development Process During the Exploratory and Establishment Stages of Black Women Attorneys, *Sex Roles*, 11(1/2), pp. 113–38.

Sly, F. (1994) Mothers in the Labour Market, *Employment Gazette*, November, p. 17.

Snapp, M.B. (1992) Occupational Stress, Social Support and Depression Among Black and White Professional-Managerial Women, *Women and Health*, 18(1), pp. 41–79.

Staines, C.L., Pleck, J.H., Shepard, L. and O'Connor, P. (1979) *Wives Unemployment Status and Marital Adjustment*, Michigan: Institute of Social Research, University of Michigan.

Stanfield, J.H. and Dennis, R.M. (Eds) (1993) *Race and Ethnicity in Research Methods*, London: Sage.

Still, L.V. (1993) *Where To From Here? The Managerial Woman in Transition*, Sydney: Business and Professional Publishing.

Sullins, E.S. (1989) Perceptual Salience as a Function of Non-Verbal Expressiveness, *Personality and Social Psychology Bulletin*, 15, pp. 584–95.

Sutherland, V. and Davidson, M.J. (1996) Managing Diversity: Using an Equal Opportunities Audit to Maximise Career Potential and Opportunities in a UK Bank, *European Journal of Work and Organisational Psychology*, 5(4), pp. 559–82.

Tannen, D. (1990) *You Just Don't Understand: Women and Men in Conversation*, New York: Melian Morris and Co.

Tarr Whelan, L. (1994) *Working Women: More Than Time for New Approaches*, Washington DC: Center for Policy Research.

Tatum, B.D. (1997) Out There Stranded? Black Families in White Communities, in H.P. McAdoo (Ed) *Black Families*, (3rd edition), London: Sage, pp. 214–33.

Terbourg, J.R. (1985) Working Women and Stress, in T.A. Beehr and R.S. Bhagat (Eds) *Human Stress and Cognition in Organisations*, Chichester: Wiley, pp. 245–86.

Terpstra, D.E. and Baker, D.D. (1991) Sexual Harassment at Work: The Psychosocial Issues, in M.J. Davidson and J.M. Earnshaw (Eds) *Vulnerable Workers – Psychosocial and Legal Issues*, Chichester: Wiley, pp. 179–202.

Thomas, D.A. (1989) Mentoring and Irrationality: The Role of Racial Taboos, *Human Resource Management*, 28(2), pp. 279–90.

Thornberg, I. (1994) Journey Toward A More Inclusive Culture, *HR Magazine*, February, pp. 79–96.

Treasure-Garwood, N. (1993) *Imani Venture*, Birmingham: Imani Venture.

Tremlett, N. and Banerji, N. (1992) *1992 Survey of Industrial Tribunals*, *Employment Gazette*, January.

US Department of Labor (1992) *Tabulations From the Current Population Surveys*, Washington DC: US Government Printing Office.

Vinnicombe, S. and Colwill, N.L. (1995) *The Essence of Women in Management*, London: Prentice Hall.

Watson, G. (1994) The Flexible Workforce and Patterns of Working Hours in the UK, *Employment Gazette*, July, pp. 239–43.

Webber, G. (1994) BBC News and Current Affairs Publicity Press Release, Panorama Survey of Top Ten Graduate Recruiters, 1983/4, Using Labour Available Figures.

Wilkinson, A. (1994) *Generations and the Gender Quake*, London: Demos.

Williams, A. (1989) Research on Black Women College Administrators: Descriptive and Interview Data, *Sex Roles*, 21(1/2), pp. 99–112.

Wilson, F. (1995) *Organizational Behaviour and Gender*, London: McGraw Hill.

White, B., Cox, C. and Cooper, C.L. (1992) *Women's Career Development – A Study of High Flyers*, Oxford: Blackwell.

White, Y.S. (1990) Understanding the Black Woman Manager's Interaction With the Corporate Culture, *The Western Journal of Black Studies*, 14(3), pp. 182–6.

Wright, P.C. and Bean, S.A. (1993) Sexual Harassment: An Issue of Employee Effectiveness, *Journal of Managerial Psychology*, 8(2), pp. 30–6.

Yaghmaiepour-Urwin, K. and Zulfiquar, M. (1994) *Mentoring For Achievement*, Leeds: Mecas Publications.

Zoltie, D. and Clarke, S. (1993) News and Views, *Women in Management Review*, 8(1), pp. 31–3.

Index